T0321803

JUST ADRIAN

Adrian Mitchell

Just Adrian

edited by Celia Mitchell and Daniel Cohen

OBERON BOOKS

LONDON

First published in 2011 by Oberon Books Ltd
521 Caledonian Road, London N7 9RH
Tel: 020 7607 3637 / Fax: 020 7607 3629
e-mail: info@oberonbooks.com
www.oberonbooks.com

We thank the following for giving us permission to quote:
Plays and Players, the *Oxford Mail*, *The Sunday Times*, *Red Pepper*,
Camden New Journal, John Fox and Peter Hulton.

A catalogue record for this book is available from the
British Library.

ISBN: 978-1-84943-047-0

Contents

I am dedicating this book to our dear generous friends Gordon and Maeve who have always been been so encouraging and supportive and without whom I might have given up the ghost long ago.

Celia Mitchell

`

Introduction

I lived with Adrian Mitchell for almost half a century and as a young actress always encouraged him to write for the theatre.

He left behind an enormous collection of papers, letters, poems and scripts of all kinds. He worked constantly, even on holiday.

When James Hogan at Oberon knew that I was going through this huge archive he suggested I make a book of his theatre writing.

So, with the help of Richard Williams, who had often directed Adrian's work, and Daniel Cohen, with his patience and tireless searching through boxes, I set about this task.

Adrian was not a writer of long convoluted essays. When he delivered an essay, it took the form of a patchwork of thoughts and comments which he would gather together on the many little note cards he always kept in his pocket, a habit he carried on throughout his life.

Sometimes these were ideas for plays and poems or notes about actors or performances he had enjoyed. Occasionally odd couplets, often very funny. They also served a very practical purpose, such as when he was trying to convince a theatre director how he would tackle the structure of a play. He would have all the scenes he might be thinking of on separate cards which he would spread out on the floor and show how they might be arranged. This method usually managed to convince the director that he was the man for the job.

So the book is a mixture of thoughts, articles, interviews and letters in which I try to give a true picture of his love of theatre, his desire to give people a good time, and to share his creative excitement with his colleagues as well as the audience.

He cannot be defined by any one style. He worked in different ways and in various media. His work includes original plays with and without music, adaptations of Spanish Golden Age and Russian classics for the Royal Shakespeare Company and the Royal National Theatre, a Beatrix Potter trilogy for children's theatre, pantomime and various site-specific events for companies like Welfare State International, Walk the Plank, a theatre on a boat, three plays for children in a Tokyo park, and a huge piece for the Woodcraft Folk's International camp in a field in Kent.

Writing is a lonely business and the theatre is a collaborative art. Adrian was a social animal and a political one. He believed in the power of poetry and theatre to change the world. This was a deeply held belief, not naïve. He knew the limits but he never lost the faith. He had a passionate belief in music theatre, in the use of song. He worked with musicians and composers of all kinds, both classical and popular. He loved working with groups of people. He enabled many such groups to create their own performances, be they children with learning difficulties or bored comprehensive school kids, university students or professional actors. He used his own extraordinary creativity unstintingly to help others. Those were his politics. He wanted to share his own excitement at the magic of theatre with everyone. And anyone who ever saw him perform cannot forget he was himself a natural performer. I hope these pieces will reflect the vitality of Adrian's mind and heart.

He would have wanted to thank all those people he worked with: all the actors he loved and the directors who made things possible. The list of those people and plays is almost endless so there is no way to thank them all. They must know how much he appreciated their art and their cooperation.

As he says in the introduction to *Love Songs of World War Three*:

'I would like to thank all my collaborators – composers, fellow-writers, actors, directors, choreographers, designers, lighting and sound people, stagehands, stage management, producers, publicists and reviewers. And my family and friends for coming to these shows and singing along.'

We thank the following for giving us permission to quote: *Plays and Players*, the *Oxford Mail*, *The Sunday Times*, *Red Pepper*, *Camden New Journal*, John Fox and Peter Hulton.

These words are about my work, which I love. I'm lucky. My true work is the making of poems, plays, song, operas, events and jokes. Sometimes I work alone. Sometimes with amateurs. Sometimes with professionals. Usually I'm paid well. I could earn more if I took dud dead theatre and telly jobs. But I'd be unhappy. I work hard and it's fun. I do it for love. I am trying to contribute to the Revolution and to the building of the New Jerusalem. 'Let me say, at the risk of seeming ridiculous, that the true revolutionary is guided by feelings of great love' – Che Guevara. Nice one.

peace
love
Adrian Mitchell

1. CHILDHOOD CASE-HISTORY

I loved my father and my mother. But I didn't want to have sex with them and they didn't want to have sex with me. They are dead, but our love goes on. I try to pass some of that love on to my children. And to you, through my writing.

2. ADULT CASE-HISTORY

I love my wife, who is a fine actress. And I love my children. Freud is up a Gum-Tree with Jehovah.

Why Go Into Theatre?

Money?

Fame?

Success?

Money – More in TV, business, whoring –

Fame – More in killing somebody famous –

Success – Tonies, Grammies, Obies, Oscars – I've been nominated for a Booby – they are just part of the advertising industry –

The Mirror – don't trust mirrors –

Good reasons:

You're very skilled and you want to use your skills and extend them.

You want to entertain people – to move them to tears and laughter.

You want to communicate with people – to give them the truth not the trash.

You have thought about the world and you have something useful to say about it.

From Adrian's archive

3. GASTODAY

I have formed an unlimited company called GASTODAY.
Stands for Glory and Song Theatre of Daft Adventures
Yes. GASTODAY prevents me from taking part in boring
undertakings and glue-mind seminars. Sing along with
Uncle Adrian:

G is for the Glory of the Golden
A is And and Amazing Animal Arts
S the Song that Soars like Buddy Bolden
T's the Theatre with a Thousand Moving Parts
O if Of and Open up Old Stories
D is Daft and likewise the reverse
A's Adventures with a rousing Chorus
Yes yank them all together they spell
GASTODAY –
GASTODAY
GASTODAY
all my troubles seemed so far away –
And GASTODAY just turned down the job
Of ruling the Multi-Verse.

The Right End of the Stick

At the *Oxford Mail* I was an over-kindly critic, too tolerant of the cult of the turgid Ugo Betti, but that stint gave me many insights into the pleasures and temptations of the drama critic's odd-shaped life. (During the day I was a general reporter dealing with fires, magistrates' courts, flower shows, brass band competitions and W. H. Auden.)

I reviewed theatrical events of all sorts. My favourites were the Cowley Amateur Dramatic Society. On my first visit a CADS lady met me at the door of the hall. There was a proscenium stage at one end, curtained decently, and many tables and chairs with candles around the hall and a bright and fully equipped bar at the other end. 'I'm the Society Press Officer. Would you like a gin and tonic?' she asked. I nodded. 'Sit down then,' and within ten seconds there were two double gin and tonics on set in front of me, and a programme. Another lady loomed up – 'Maybe you'd like a bottle of wine to follow, white or red, I'm the director,' and suddenly I faced an open bottle of white in an ice bucket. And so on.

The curtain went back on some murder mystery. There was a sofa, three or four chairs and a large, fully operational cocktail cabinet. A maidservant entered to answer the convincingly ringing phone. To the silent receiver she outlined the list of characters who would soon be Murder Suspects. Gradually they began to enter – starting with the Host, a red-faced and cheery engineer. As each guest entered he would ask them what they would like to drink and try to satisfy their alcoholic whims. Every now and then the dialogue would be interrupted by some character saying: 'Why don't we have another drink?' and everybody would fill their glasses.

It soon became clear to the bleariest observer that the cast were enjoying real drinks, free drinks, lavishly dispensed and hastily dispatched. The mood was catching.

Halfway through the first half I had to visit the gents, returning to find that my white wine had been renewed by the play's director. At the interval the Society Press Officer brought me two more large gin and tonics.

During the second act those who had moustaches or beards were losing them. The audience was also well supplied and rollicking with mirth at any joke or mistake. You could always tell the mistakes because the guilty actor would say 'sorry'. At the end everybody cheered. It was a staggering success.

I refused a post-show party and, after two falls in a hundred yards, used my bike as a Zimmer frame to carry me back to the Office. I stared at my typewriter hopelessly. Then I shrugged to myself. I'd had a great evening. The cast had a great evening. The audience had a great evening. Great! I began to type: 'It was a thoroughly enjoyable evening...'

Perhaps I was getting The Right End of the Stick?

From Adrian's archive

4. I'M A WITCH DOCTOR

Ted Hughes, our greatest living poet, doesn't read the critics, ever. Bloody right. There have always been poets because poems are necessary. I suppose there have always been people who know better than poets but they've only recently found a title – Critic.

Joan Littlewood

Comedy in England is too often infected with the drawing-room virus, the polite cough and the refined sneeze. A comedy without restraint, and with more (concealed) point than most of the West End's 'problem plays' is *The Good Soldier Schweik*, presented at the Playhouse all this week by Theatre Workshop.

The play traces the private's progress of a gormless Czech in the first World War, from the moment when he learns of the assassination of some Archduke at Sarajevo to the moment when he sees his friends die pointlessly at the front. Schweik is played with ease as a lanky, wondering simpleton by Maxwell Shaw.

Faced with a charge of high treason or a ferociously drastic medical treatment, Schweik swings into his subversive salute and grins happily. Confronted with such blankness, authority must be discomfited, and Schweik is never so much in command of the situation as when he is being reprimanded.

Perhaps the finest scene at the Playhouse last night was the line of decrepit soldiers waiting on church parade. Standing at attention, in fear of an officer presumably stationed in the stalls, each man muttered out of the corner of his mouth, passing the message down the line until Schweik appeared.

He made his way into the centre of the rank and started to talk in his friendly, artless way, and when warned of authority attempted to imitate his comrades.

This was only called to a halt by the appearance of the drunken padre, played with boozy irreverence by Gerry Raffles. The sermon which followed, with its ripe condemnation of the troops for scratching when they itched, moved Schweik to tears and the audience to wild laughter.

This is the funniest production in Oxford for a long time. Lulled to a half-sleep by the smooth under-acting of today's stars, audiences are woken up without ceremony by a cartoon style of acting, and by the use of the word cartoon no lack of subtlety is implied.

The ladies especially have the vitality to set the theatre on fire, and the company gives the play all the enthusiasm it needs and deserves.

This is a comedy for the low-brow, a satire for the high-brow, and a wonderful production for all those in between. It is refreshing and entirely enjoyable, for Schweikervessence lasts the whole play through.

Originally published in the Oxford Mail, *27 June 1956*

Theatre Workshop:
The Word Spreads

By Wednesday evening Theatre Workshop's brilliant *The Good Soldier Schweik* was playing to double its scanty first night audience at the Playhouse. Word had passed round that this was a company with something new to offer.

Next Wednesday the company will be in Paris, to play four nights in the biggest theatre in the city, and will then return to play in Brendan Behan's *The Quare Fellow* in the Comedy Theatre, London.

The Workshop began with £300 and a number of manifestoes. Joan Littlewood and Gerald Raffles founded a group which had some beliefs in common; virile acting and group work were the rule and still are.

These and other principles, put into practice over eight and a half years of touring and successive seasons at the Stratford Theatre in the East End of London, are substantially unaltered.

Here are some of the beliefs, from Miss Littlewood and Mr. Raffles:

'The theatre should present the conscience and the history of the people.

'A company should be capable of all styles, including circus and vulgarity.

'The idea is not just a company but a centre where

artists, writers, actors and musicians can come and work.

'The first job is to find out the truth of the play, what the author had in mind.

'The greatest theatre involves song, dance and movement.

'Anyone who wants to write for the theatre should come and work in a theatre.'

It has been a struggle to keep the Workshop open since 1945, but the actors have remained optimistic even when living (literally) on porridge.

Each artist is paid the same wage, the only variation being for family allowances. And each artist is prepared to help by working in his or her spare time to earn for the company.

Actors are expected to think for themselves, to do research into their parts, to improvise and to observe people in pubs, buses and meetings.

In Paris Theatre Workshop is widely regarded as the best British company. Its visit next week is to represent Great Britain at the Paris International Theatre Festival.

On their home ground, Stratford, the company are truly popular, and their policy of strong drama, new and controversial plays, and vivid acting has won them a fervent audience.

At the first night of Ibsen's *Enemy of the People* there was almost a free fight as the audience took sides, for Theatre Workshop demands and gets strong reactions wherever it goes.

Originally published in the Oxford Mail, *29 June 1956*

Joan Littlewood, who died recently, was one of our greatest artists. She wasn't just a great theatre director, but a visionary who tried to transform society. She certainly changed millions of lives. As a young theatre critic on the *Oxford Mail* I was very excited and inspired by her production of *The Good Soldier Schweik*. I grabbed the chance to interview Joan and her beloved partner Gerry Raffles for as long as I could. When they had to leave for rehearsals, I asked my last – rather transparent – question: 'Miss Littlewood, what should someone do who wants to work in the theatre?' She looked at me with a lopsided grin: 'Come and join us, doll,' she said. One of the few regrets of my life is that I didn't have the nerve.

But I went to her shows and delighted in her work and watched her influence spread and spread over actors and writers and audiences. Her heart was broken twice – by the early death of Gerry Raffles and by the bureaucrats who prevented her Fun Palace from being built just when it seemed to have triumphed. In her last years I asked her, as everybody did, if she wouldn't direct some more plays in England. 'I've done two hundred bloody years in the theatre,' she said. 'That's enough, isn't it?' You can see the effects of that work in action wherever British theatre is honest and treats its audience as equals – especially at London's Theatre Royal, Stratford East.

The name Littlewood was far too small for her – it suggests a little copse. But Joan was great. Her surname should have been Bloody-Great-Jungle-Full-Of-Fucking-Chimpanzees.

Originally published in Red Pepper, *November 2002 issue*

5. ADMISSION FREE BUT TAKE
YOUR SOCKS OFF IF YOU LIKE

Theatre should be free in all senses. Theatre's about liberation. 'If you don't pay for it you don't value it' – too right, Greyface, just like sex, just like a birthday present, just like love, just like a meal with your friends in a house of bright colours. Art is a gift. Theatre is an exchange of gifts. Raise the money by jumble sales, taxes, sponsored massage – but make it Admission Free. Changes the nature of your audience. You get kids coming in and they keep coming back if they like it at all and their responses are honest and clear and direct to put it mildly. The new audience changes the nature of your work.

On Writing for Performance

When you became involved in theatre – the ability to listen to an audience, the ability to make contrasts, presumably gave you an idea of what theatre performance could be.

Yes it must have done. There's a big difference between being an actor and doing what I do. In my case it's a question of utter belief – there is no pretending. It is risky in that sense. What I believe and what I'm fighting for is on the line every time. With an actor that may happen. He may find a poem or a play that he absolutely believes in, that reflects his soul and what he's living for. But it doesn't often happen because an actor has to pretend. If a play fails it's not such a personal matter, it shouldn't be so drastic. A whole team shares the failure. If I do a solo poetry reading and it fails, then it's my fault and I feel grim.

When did you start working with young people in terms of group writing?

In 1965 at the Bradford College of Art, a project called *Bradford Walk*. This was the first time I'd got together with a group to write something – the course was called 'Making Poetry Public'. I had a group of Bradford Art Students for ten days. We spent the first day just talking about Bradford and they tried to scare me with things like 'You cross your legs in a Bradford pub and you'll get cut up'. I said what do you want to do and their immediate reaction was that they wanted to get out of the place and onto the Moors. I said if we went everyone was to take a notebook and from the moment we left the college were to make reference points like 'Beginning of bus journey' and 'End of bus journey', 'Walk to first gate' etc. This was so that we would know where we were in retrospect.

I suggested we listen to conversations around us and watch and see what could be seen. We were hearing these odd things that people were saying and noting them down. That's basic training in writing anyway – you learn that people say much more interesting things than writers often give them credit for. 'Naturalistic' writers tend to normalise things, to cut out the imaginative weirdness of real live people. I didn't know what would come of this and said drop your note-taking at times and just dig the walk. It was a wonderful walk. We finished up in a pub and they gave me the notebooks. We decided as it was a good walk we'd try to do a show about it which we'd present at the end of ten days, just to friends, because I didn't think we'd be ready to take it any further than that.

The form the piece took was that we reconstructed the walk, we had a bus, there was a little stage which we used as the ridge we walked across on the moor, and the audience was in the middle of our walk. Every so often we'd stop the walk and somebody would do a poem or song they'd written, for instance, a song about a local eccentric whom we had talked about called 'The Hermit'. The audience were given posters and wine and finished up with armfuls of presents. Then we all went to the pub and drank with our legs apart. I think it was the most successful show I worked on in its simple way. Many of these students worked with Albert Hunt regularly.[1]

And your second group experience?

That was *US* with the RSC at the Aldwych which has been pretty well documented. It ended in a clash between Liberals on the one hand and Socialists/ Anarchists on the other. I was on the losing side, being a Socialist and an Anarchist.

---

1 Albert Hunt was a much-admired teacher at the Bradford Regional College of Art, where he ran the Bradford Art College Theatre Group. He has also written on theatre and organised happenings.

In what way was that a group-writing piece?

Well, it started off with the group contribution being the idea. I suppose you could say the First Act was a group-written show (the Second Act was almost all the work of Denis Cannan with a few songs by Dick Peaslee and myself thrown in. I hated the Second Act because though it was powerful, it wasn't about the war, it was irrelevant). In Act One we decided on scenes we wanted and different people did them, and they were put together in a kind of patchwork-quilt structure, which I think is the best structure of all. At least it is my favourite structure for a group-written show. You decide on a story line, agree on that, and then you map out areas and make a scenario. When you have a scenario you go around asking who would like to do which scene. This is not how it happened in *US*, but how it would be in a group piece that I was running. The idea is to keep the story moving – the characters must move from A to D but your style is your own. That way you end up with a show with a surrealist scene, a realistic scene, operatic, depending on the motivation of each writer. Everybody invents a style and part of the fun comes from the contrast of those styles.

You always have a great deal of script editing to do. First you read out a scene that has been written in the group and people comment on it and then you try it out. Maybe the writer sees what's wrong with it if there is anything wrong with it. And then the script editor talks to the person about their scene to suggest ways in which it might be improved – these changes are not spelt out but are just suggestions for tightening. Part of the aim of these shows is to teach people how to write and one of the things you can teach is the importance of rewriting. But while they're rewriting you don't make them conform to what you think is good writing. You try and encourage them to go their own way, although there are certain ground rules like getting rid of clichés. On the other hand if someone writes a lot of puns which I personally can't stand, I wouldn't object to their inclusion, as long as they're good ones. That's patchwork quilt. It's a bit like poetry reading in that it works by contrast. You try to arrange it so there aren't two consecutive scenes with the same characteristics.

When people come to watch these group shows – would it be true that they are less likely to get lost as long as the storyline is clear?

You have to choose the right sort of story. You can't take any story and work in this way. You want an episodic story for a start. This is jumping ahead chronologically, but at Lancaster we worked on a dramatisation of *The Odyssey* called *Lash Me to the Mast* which was ideal because our source was a series of adventures. We linked it together by including Homer. Greg Stevens invented this and it was our second show there. The first was one I suggested called *The Hot Pot Saga*, which was a race war between Yorkshire and Lancashire – it was developed soon after Enoch Powell had made his famous 'Rivers of Blood' speech, so there was something of that going on underneath the main scenario. It had a basic Panto format with Young Jack, a pop singer coming back from London to Lancashire with a very big head – it began amusingly and got very black and frightening towards the end. In Panto form you can do all kinds of different things, including tragedy.

The clearer the narrative, the further away from the story you can move, because the audience are still with you through the power of the story, even though you might have moved out into a wild area.

Yes, for example in *Lash Me to the Mast* we had Boris and Maggie Howarth working with us from Welfare State International theatre group, and they chose to rework the scene where Ulysses comes back and his old dog runs out to him and dies.[2] I said that's fine. Boris

2   Boris and Maggie Howarth were founder members, with John Fox, of the alternative theatre company Welfare State International. See p.96 'John Fox and Welfare State International'.

said, 'look, I've changed the dog to a worm and it's got twenty-two legs – you've got eleven actors spare'. So we had this incredible worm with more than twenty-two legs, everyone wanted to be part of it, it danced onto the stage to this gloomy song. It was somehow meant to be Ulysses' dog coming out to meet him. I'm not sure whether anyone in the audience quite knew what was going on. It was wonderful to look at – a great black worm with 22, 24, 28 legs dancing round and then collapsing with joy at the sight of Ulysses. The work at Lancaster included professional actors who happened to be there at the time – they taught everyone a lot, of course.

The idea of Free Theatre evolved during the work on *Lash Me to the Mast* at Lancaster. Maggie and Boris said they wanted to make admission to the show free. First people asked how that was possible. We'd already hired a theatre in the centre of Lancaster (where Sarah Bernhardt once played) and we didn't have much money and we had to do publicity, etc. Boris and Maggie said 'well, we're not doing it if you charge money'. We realised we needed Boris and Maggie more than the money and set about working out ways of raising money. We had a huge jumble sale which made a lot of money and a rock concert. And that way we made enough for the show.

The theatre backed on to the slums of Lancaster and

there were a lot of kids who didn't have anywhere to go. They saw us go in and out with masks and funny stuff and they started coming in. The feeling of the group was to let them watch – they brought their friends and friends' friends and we soon had an audience for every rehearsal. We could see that they'd come to every performance because it was free. We knew we had to please those guys and some of them were quite tough. When we had long discussion scenes on stage they'd get bored, run around and muck up the lights. We had to take responsibility for that – were we going to bore the audience with that long scene that the kids didn't understand? So we tried to make the whole show so they'd be engaged and not bored.

That was the first free theatre I did. We did a variation later at Billericay where we said 'don't bring money, but bring a chocolate bar.' In the play the Intergalactic Cup gets stolen and when it's restored at the climax of the play they open it and find it's full of chocolate bars which are handed out to the audience. Either way it's really free theatre and it seems to change the nature of the audience. Some people don't come because it's free theatre and some people do come because it's free theatre. Some regular theatregoers say 'well, you don't value it if you don't pay for it.' I say to them: 'Yeah… like love.' Ultimately it was very good for us all, even those who initially objected to having kids at rehearsals. And it's an imaginative step towards the abolition of money.

I always take my kids to everything I write and wouldn't write anything I couldn't take them to. In *Lash Me to the Mast* there was a love song with the word 'breasts' in and the kids didn't muck around in that – they liked it – a good song, well sung. There was an argument scene – Ulysses arguing with a Lord of an Island. It was a political scene, but they didn't mind because there was a dynamism to it. They weren't bored by that because it was a real argument. They could follow the story through that too. But there was a philosophical scene that they got fed up with. They were right, it didn't work dramatically. I could read it and enjoy it, but sitting and watching it, no.

In 1968 there was the dramatisation of the Old Testament that Albert Hunt and I worked on – *Move over Jehovah* or *The Man who shot Emily Bronte*. That was with a group of students from Bradford with Albert, with John Fox and Boris and Maggie Howarth again. Maggie was working on design and John Fox concentrated on the programme, which was a monster programme – a huge bag with pieces of paper and carpet and leaves. The National Association for Mental Health asked Albert and me to devise a group-written show for a Conference of International Psychiatrists. We talked with them a lot and decided on the Old Testament as a subject because we thought with Moses and Aaron in charge of the children of Israel, whom we saw as mental patients, we could devise a piece about Authority. Their main task was to stop the children touching each other. Above them we had the Trinity in Heaven, Jehovah as a group captain with a lot of medals and a smiting machine – with levers for lice, boils and leprosy. When the flood came Jesus would look down and say 'Look, daddy, there's a little lamb' – he was a bit wet. The Holy Ghost wore an Italian suit and shades he was going to take over – he smoked black cigarettes. And then there was Lucifer who, for some reason, was a girl in hot pants, a typist. Everyone took a different scene. Jonah was quite a spectacle – what it's like to be swallowed by a whale. It was one immense performance of about three and a half hours. We'd arranged that when they came out of Holland Park Comprehensive, which was where it was done, we'd hired a man with a camel to stand outside in the playground, to finally freak them. The Old Testament – a camel. He never showed – he got caught in the traffic at Notting Hill Gate. That was my one regret about the show.

There were some good things about puritanism etc. An example of a serious scene was The Death of Noah, which was mostly based on the death of my father. Another was Adam and Eve discovering – with delight – each others' bodies. The Trinity were a comic relief. The heroes were the Children of Israel – a subversive mob. We put it together in four weeks, which isn't bad for the Old Testament. The importance of this kind of work for me is not just the end product, the show (which is very important – not just sitting round in a writing group and reading it to each other, but to have something to show other people at the end of it), but the working together, the discussions, learning to fit scaffolding. You learn by doing not theorising.

How do you go about recruiting the group?

That's always a difficult one. I do it through readings and vulgar publicity. Photostatted, noisy posters. We always found it difficult to get group games going. I'm physically inhibited in that way. I always prefer to work with a director from the beginning so we can have trust games, etc. I can play but can't initiate those. One way of getting people to write when they're stuck in groups and one way to clarify the writing when they are trying to appear more intellectual than they are, which was my problem for a long time, is to get them to write for specific children. To think of Judy aged six and write some poems for her, and give them to Judy aged six.

That helps loosen people up, especially people who are writing very agonised things, because they are scared about nuclear war, like I am, but they just have this agony going round and round and eating them up and they can't do anything else. If they have to write for children, they have to find more life in their verse.

Then in 1974 and 1976 there were two group projects at Dartington College of Arts: *Mass Media Mash* was a piece where the studio was covered in newspapers. It was a day in the life of the Mass Media. We took one day and we studied it for what the newspapers said, what the magazines said, what the radio said, what the TV said – we all monitored a whole day. What they said – and what they meant. We chose stories we liked and which fascinated us. The structure was based on two people, both concerned with the mass media, living through a day in their life. They didn't know each other. I think they had one second's contact during the day. One was a rich owner of a newspaper, incredibly wealthy, and the other was a woman who sold newspapers.

The other was the infamous eight-hour *Mud Fair* on The Island of Angels. That came about because we wanted to do something outside the college and we wanted to do something for kids. The idea was to have an all-day, eight-hour show which would be made up of sideshows and plays and operas and games, things happening simultaneously, but no money. It was a very cold day – we'd had to spend the previous night on the island with some braziers which we'd learnt to make. There were things going on in different parts of the island – a very complicated operation, events in each corner and then we'd gather everyone for a big event like the beauty contest.

The *Mud Fair* included many different acts and sideshows: two brief operas, a mock beauty contest, a speech of great pomposity, a number of brief plays both comic and tragic, dances, mud-flinging competitions, Dennis the Menace and his Gang, an escapologist, puppets, free hot refreshments, fortune-telling, the Jumblies in a boat, fireworks and a dance of ghosts. (There were plenty of other attractions.) You judge an event like a fair, you go along for a few hours and if you have a good time then it's good. It was more like a fair than a play. Both projects were exhausting. With *Mass Media Mash* I was scripting, editing and directing. Far too much. William York, the composer, helped with the *Mud Fair* a great deal.

How do you get people writing in these projects?
In the case of a school like Billericay there were kids who were keen on writing and they volunteered to participate. In other cases it has been different. When

I was at Cardiff as Resident Writer at the Sherman Theatre for two terms (1975-76), I was teaching a theatre course and was told that I could teach what I wanted. I couldn't build the writing group out of that as a lot of them didn't want to write anyway. Despite a lot of publicity the students were working just too hard to want to write. I found there was a bookshop called the '108 bookshop', a community bookshop, a sort of headquarters for radicals and local activists in all sorts of fields. I went to them and told them I'd been promised the main theatre for three nights for free where we could put on anything we liked – one of the conditions being that we couldn't charge any admission fee.

These people were interested and there were people from the Gypsy Action Group, the Housing Action Group and so on. Just as we thought we might not have enough people the Women's Action Group came in and they were tremendous – they had the Battered Wives' Group etc. The moment we thought we had the gang together the Campaign for Homosexual Equality came along and joined us. The main context for the work was that we should speak for those who normally had no voice.

These groups wanted to do agitprop scenes with songs. We had a very good songwriter there called Geoff Pearson whom I worked with in Cardiff for the first time. The obvious danger was that the whole thing would be incredibly gloomy but these people wanted to write because they had something to say, something they knew about. I was aware it could end up being an oppressive moan about the terrible conditions that exist in Cardiff and elsewhere and that the audience would come out desolate and tired. So we invented a structure which was a National Conference of People in Power. The people in power were summoned to give an account of themselves and in the eccentric nature of this conference they had to act out their failures. There was a person in charge of persecuting gypsies, a person in charge of making sure poor people stayed in slums, someone in charge of making life difficult for gays. So they had to act out their failures. Each scene represented a victory for the people. They were little victories but that was the emphasis – to show a gypsy fighting back and actually winning against a sheriff, a gay finding brothers that cared, a battered woman who actually broke away. We pushed the stories towards that. They were serious stories with jokes and songs but within this satirical structure.

All the people in power had blazers and straw hats. They were played by the same people who appeared later in sketches as ordinary people. They weren't professional actors. Not only did they have blazers and straw hats but they all walked with a limp of the left leg. (Most of them had never been on stage before, so this was a rough acting technique to give them a kind of ridiculous ultra-conformity – The Limp.)

An example of the way the writing was developed occurred in the Women's Action Group. They were working on a scene about a woman being beaten. It was being presented in almost abstract language, they were shouting clichés at each other, but you didn't remember anything afterwards. John Roche, the director, said: 'who is this based on' and they said: 'a girl who lives down the street', he said: 'what did she actually say', she said: 'he said he'd break the neck off a bottle and dip it in red pepper and stick it up her cunt'. John said, 'well you've got to say that and then people will remember it forever'. She had held back because it seemed a bit much. Well it's terrifying – but it is true. With the gays there was a series of scenes about this guy and his difficulties in Cardiff (it's not an easy city to be gay in). We linked the scenes with a narrative song which he sang – and then the narrative would be carried forward, he'd walk into a scene and act it and then come out and sing. He began with:

'I'd like to tell a story, a story that is true,
If you'll kindly listen to it you might see my point of view
I am a homosexual and one of the human race
But I hung my head and hid my face.'

43

The first night he did that in a spotlight it got a terrible laugh from a couple of hearties, but he just kept singing it, he fixed on them and just sang it. The audience were won over by his courage in a matter of seconds. Their sketch ended with them inviting gays from the audience to come on the stage and dance with them – which people did every night in Cardiff, which took some courage. There were many triumphs – first we were just acting in our own sketches, and gradually everybody merged until you forgot what group they had come from. A lot of people kept in touch and went on to use more sketches and songs in their day-to-day fight and demonstrations. They were a great group – working hard all day at their own jobs, and then coming to make this in their evenings.

… The relationship between the people who are doing it and the material they're presenting, the homosexual and his story, the kids in Bradford and their story, there is something moving about that close link between the performer and his work.

I feel that about these shows. It would be silly to show people scripts and say why don't you do the *Hot Pot Saga* and *Cardiff Rules OK* – they came out of our experience together.

Have you used this group writing device with younger children in schools?

Yes I have – at Billericay Comprehensive in Essex where I was Visiting Writer for two years (1978-80). I formed a group to write first and they were working on a variety of individual projects, and they seemed interested in science fiction, soccer and rock. I invented a thing called the *Intergalactic Cup*, which was set in the year 5000 AD, where Billericay's soccer team (mixed boys and girls) has won the World Cup ten years running and therefore qualifies for the Intergalactic Cup. That means it has to play a series of knock-out matches on various planets.

After we'd fixed on this idea we started inventing characters for the team, and then we invented some villainesses who were fighting against the Billericay team. Someone invented the idea of the Space Coach, which was a very ratty little rocket which the team travelled around in. So that was the main direction of the piece. And then everyone invented a planet – one girl invented thirty-two planets but most invented one planet with population, gravity, flora and fauna. And we told each other about our planets. We each wrote a story about the soccer team coming to the planet and the next stage was to try to dramatise that, which was harder. I'd get together with each writer and work on their scene. There were two teachers involved and it went down to twelve-year-olds. I think the older ones learnt something from the little ones who were amazing. The show was helped by having a very naïve episode next to a very knowing 'science fiction buffs' scene. We presented it and it was rough but we brought a lot of goodwill to it. You have to, it's not like a professional show which just knocks you out. There's never enough time, there's always a rush.

Houdini was an opera you made in 1977 – was he someone you wanted to write about?

Peter Schat, the Dutch composer, suggested it first as an opera. Peter had set two of my poems to music and he wanted to do his trying to get in contact with his mother when she was dead, and the similarities with Orpheus who also tried to get in contact with his mother when she died. So there was a kind of Orpheus there in Houdini. We both liked Houdini a lot. Peter and I are both interested in a kind of opera where if you are deaf you can still enjoy it, because there is so much spectacle and so much happening. I think in the last production in Amsterdam they really got that feeling. There were big scenes and little scenes alternating – intimate scenes with an oven and an apron and a few coins, and then a big scene with crowds moving around, a circus in front of your eyes or a ship leaving for Europe. There were big public scenes and private scenes.

Did you have a clear idea of script and music before rehearsals began?

Oh yes, I'd finished my work then. I was just watching points of interpretation during rehearsal. The libretto was written. Once Peter and I had agreed on the sweep of the story I went away and wrote summaries of about 30 possible scenes, shuffled them around into an order, threw out a lot of them, thought I'd got an order and took it back to Peter. We agreed then what it should be, but then things would happen at the last moment. Peter found a newspaper article that said that they had discovered a letter from Houdini which he wrote near the end of his life when he was very successful, he had written to the man in charge of coal mine safety in America explaining that some of the miners who got trapped in the coal mines could survive if they followed particular rules and he gave a series of rules about breathing and conservation of air which would keep them alive ten times as long. We were both very impressed that Houdini, who by this time you might have thought would be in show business heaven, should take the time to do that. Peter said if we could find a way he'd like to set the letter to music so we had a little scene in a dressing room where Houdini's wife was reading the letter back to Houdini. They sing it together and he shows her the breathing exercise – that's just before his death. We didn't want to say one thing about Houdini, we wanted to say a lot of things and that added another dimension to the work.

So you identify a storyline and then assemble the possible scenes which can hold the storyline and then get into writing the individual scenes.

It tends to be more if I have a subject like Houdini, Mark Twain or Blake I go through all their work and find possible scenes first, rather than a storyline – I don't know what storyline is. It's a very wasteful way of going about business. Generally the storyline comes later. It was certainly like that with Blake and Houdini. With Houdini we used a chronology, there were things developing through those scenes but I don't know if you could say it had a plot. It was more episodic than that. I go for scenes because they're stories in themselves. I like those little anecdotes about Blake – when he was reading *Paradise Lost* with his wife naked in the garden, and a friend came in and got all embarrassed and headed for the garden door and Blake said, 'Come on in it's only Adam and Eve'. Nowadays some Blake scholars can't imagine this actually happened – well I can. I think it's great. I believe and love those stories about people.

Do you hear a lot of music in your work?

Some of it's about music. I wrote *Hoagy Bix and Wolfgang Beethoven Bunkhaus* which has been done twice in America since the Wakefield Tricycle tour in 1980. It was about music, about friendship and about loss. It breaks a lot of rules. I like it a lot. There's hardly any conflict in it, there's nobody really bad in the play – they all like each other with a little bit of difficulty. But the enemies tend to be the pressure of work, commercialism, booze etc. The enemies aren't people. (I'm fantastically against people when they say you can't change human nature.) They performed it beautifully. It's been done in the States in Indianapolis and the Mark Taper in L.A.

My tribute plays aren't just songbook compilations. They try to show something of the how and why an honest artist can survive in a corrupt society. I want to send the audience back to the artist with new or renewed excitement.

Have you directed any of this professional work?

No. I like working with directors. I sit and make

notes and deliver them complicated memos the next morning to read when they've got time. We usually stay on good terms.

Do you see the scenes happening on stage as you are writing?

I didn't at first, but now more and more. With *Hoagy* I included a lot of visual instructions that I never used to do – the colours of their costumes, the different areas of the stage. I did a script for *Hoagy* with lots of pictures to give the mood of a scene. I cut up reproduction catalogues of the twenties and photostatted them, it made the script more fun to read.

I'm always writing pieces with songs. I was lucky with the Oxford Playhouse where we did *Peer Gynt* with songs by Nick Bicat, a lot of the cast for that could sing and play instruments. I did a verse version of the play with songs. I hope it will be done again, but there are so many *Peer Gynts* around. As the RSC are doing *Peer Gynt* with David Rudkin, the National won't be doing it for a while. At Oxford we had fifteen or sixteen in the cast. I always work from a literal translation. The theatre gets somebody to this, in the case of *Peer Gynt* it was Karin Bamborough from the National Theatre. Karin did a literal translation, word for word with explanations and notes and points about the verse.

Then she read me some in Norwegian so I could get the sound, and I worked from there.

One of the decisions with *Peer Gynt* was that Ibsen gives you a free hand by saying, 'Oh they're going to stage my poem, well cut down Act Four and do it as a series of tableaux', but we wanted to keep the sweep of that, keep just about all the scenes but make them shorter and use songs to condense very long speeches. The idea was to retain the picaresque quality, its sense of movement so even Ralph Steadman could sit through it. We updated some references – to the Trolls particularly, who we recast as a 'Me Generation' group –

Men say: 'To thine own self be true.'
Trolls say: 'Me first! And right up you!'

There was a rock number called 'Me First':

Sir Philip Sidney on the battlefield lay
He was badly wounded in the heat of the day.
He saw a fellow-soldier who was dying of thirst
So he grabbed the guy's Heineken yelling: Me first!
Me first
When they ladle out the honey
Me first
When they handing out the money

If they're standing in line
I'll be round the back door
Me first, me first
Till there isn't any more
If I'm gonna be first
I gotta be fast
Only suckers finish last
So I'll do my best
And I'll do my worst
The result?
Me first, me first, me first.

The Troll King was a kind of ageing hippy/guru, he was at a terrible disco. That was the only part of the play in which we did that kind of updating. We thought the trolls were out of time anyway. I adapted the scene with the monkeys. Gordon MacDougall said he wasn't sure we should have the scene with the monkeys – I said hang on, you don't pass up the chance of a scene with monkeys. In our version, Peer gets chased up a tree by a lion and is just saying 'yah boo, Lion' when a whole load of monkeys start throwing shit on his head from the top of the tree. It's such a light-hearted play anyway – Ibsen was living in Frascati when he wrote it and I think he was hitting it a bit. It's a lovely play. I would never have wanted to do *Brand* anyway. Geoffrey Hill has done that. I like doing light-hearted plays.

A piece like *Peer Gynt* was mainly to do with translation. I generally work very fast – partly for deadlines, partly for economic reasons. *Peer Gynt* took four weeks including verse and songs. With *The Mayor of Zalamea* it was the same. I had a very good literal translation of that with a lot of notes. When I was commissioned to do it I'd never read a Spanish play of that era. I read it for the first time and I thought yes I know that guy Crespo. I lived in the Yorkshire Dales for five years and knew some farmers up there. I took their rhythm of speech and put it on Crespo. That line 'How's loitering?' – that's Yorkshire.

I'm doing more work with the National now. *The Government Inspector* with Richard Eyre and I'm going to do some Spanish plays. *The Mayor of Zalamea* was a play I liked as soon as I read it. I have been asked to do plays, for instance *The Misanthrope*, where I had to say, 'I don't see a way of doing it, I'm not very interested or excited by it, if you want to get the second-best couplet writer in the country you ought to ask Tony Harrison'. Tony is a wonderful poet, I knew he worked in the theatre in Africa. Now *The Oresteia* and *Mayor of Zalamea* are in repertory at the same time.

What challenges faced you working on The Mayor of Zalamea?

Writing in syllabic verse which I'd never done before. It had always struck me as being a bit silly. I count on my fingers – walking up and down. I enjoy doing syllabic verse but it presents a real problem for the critics. People wrote 'well this stuff doesn't scan'. Syllabic verse doesn't scan, it goes on speech rhythms. Or they'd say 'this doesn't rhyme' – but there are deliberate half rhymes, assonances, as Calderón uses himself. Some of the time there would be full-frontal rhyme.

Did you have to change the play in any way?

There was a change in that there are two acts instead of three. I didn't do that. It should be three acts. The Calderón structure demands three acts. Some material was cut but not much.

When Foco Novo asked me to adapt *A Seventh Man* in 1976 I had felt quite different about that adaptation. Originally I had made a couple of scenes that were in a political cartoon style, personified rich nations sitting around in masks – but that came out. Nobody liked those scenes except me. I had known John Berger beforehand, he had reviewed a book of my poems and we got to know each other. There are things which just leap out of the book: the photographs, the description in the abattoir, a weird little scene of a guy visiting a prostitute. What I tried to add – which comes in the book but not as often as I felt necessary – is the way people like that fight back and survive by using jokes. So I gave them more jokes. There's a joker in there making jokes about the doctor. I felt that was necessary for several reasons. For me sitting in the audience it helped me as well as for them, their surviving. I wanted them to have that kind of resilience and humour.

I felt happier working on a lot of other shows because in this case I think it's a great book and I felt very responsible for getting it on as much like the book as possible. But when you feel you've got a duty then it's a bit heavier. I didn't feel that with *Peer Gynt*. I thought: there are lots of *Peer Gynts* and my version is just one among many *Peer Gynts*. I'm really going to enjoy this and Ibsen said I could – so Frascati here we go. I also took some liberties with *The Mayor of Zalamea*. Soon after *A Seventh Man* I formed a company in my head called GASTODAY which stands for Glory and Song Theatre of Daft Adventures Yes. If someone approached me with a job I thought I should do for political reasons or any other reason like that I'd go to GASTODAY and sometimes GASTODAY would say 'No, too heavy-hearted'. I like fighting but with a light heart, I don't want to drag people down. I don't mean not being serious. But I have to answer to GASTODAY.

Have you got any one way of attacking the writing for a stage performance other than going back to the book or scenes?

It's always different. I generally do far more reading and writing than I need. For *Mowgli's Jungle* which I did with Manchester Contact, for instance, which is based on the *Jungle Books*, I got quite scared of it because I couldn't find a structure. I bought lots of books about wolves and sat there reading them, while the real problem was how to shape it. I broke through when I got the idea of having two Mowglis – a little boy Mowgli and an eighteen-year-old adolescent Mowgli. I was able to use this dramatically to show the growing up as a big moment, maybe at the end of Act 1. That was a breakthrough because I could then see it was partly about growing up – the First Act would be about Mowgli and the animals where he is learning to be part of the jungle but is not part of the jungle. The Second Act would be more concerned with Mowgli going to the people and trying and finding he is not a person. That's part of the fascination with Mowgli where he realises he is not jungle and he's not village, he's not people and he's not beast – he's Mowgli. That's why it's so exciting. That was how the breakthrough came.

In a Mowgli story called 'In the Rukh' (which isn't in the *Jungle Books*) there's a Forest Officer who has a comic Indian servant, and the Forest Officer offers Mowgli a job helping him in the jungle – with pension. But Mowgli falls in love with the comic servant's daughter and they go off into the jungle. There's a scene where the comic servant comes across them, she's lying down and Mowgli playing his flute and the wolf is dancing on his hind legs. This freaks the comic servant and you're meant to make a lot of fun of the comic servant as his daughter's been seduced. I thought I'm not going to do that one. So I gave the Forest Officer, played by Richard Williams, Mr Barnstaple, a daughter called Daisy Barnstaple – she was a bit simple. And I gave her a book by Edward Lear and she sang 'Calico Pie', which is one of my favourite poems. And Mowgli fell in love with her and it all came back on the forest officer. Kipling wouldn't have liked that. And then there was a happy ending.

If you don't crack the shaping process you're just left with a lot of scenes. It happens in my novels too. With *The Bodyguard* I must have written 45 episodes and used about 20. I don't know what order they're going to be in when I write. I know one thing about it though.

When I've been asked by people to write a synopsis – a detailed synopsis for a TV play or something – I really hate it, because I think once I've done that it's boring to write it. Once I know what's going to happen it's not very interesting, the adventure goes. If you know exactly where it is going and why people are doing it then all you've got to write out is what they're wearing, how they say 'I'm not going to kill you after all' – we might as well go home. It's no fun. I was working on a piece recently where they wanted the synopsis first. I resisted, they insisted that they wanted another synopsis and more discussion. What we ended up with was four synopses – each one more painful to write than the one before.

When I wrote *Man Friday* for TV the synopsis was eight lines long and they commissioned it on the strength of that. Again with *Man Friday* I wrote lots of scenes and didn't know which order they'd be in. I worked that out later and adjusted the stream running through. In an ideal situation I would like to be at each rehearsal to shuffle scenes around. I did it rather too much with *Hoagy*. Everyone has ideas as to how they think that play should be – then it becomes too flexible. In good circumstances things change during the process. One of the nicest instances of this was knowing I would be working with Liverpool Everyman in 1973 and seeing four company shows in a row. I knew I had Jonathan Pryce and Tony Sher and Bernard Hill with Alan Dossor directing. I knew I was working for a gifted company and in watching the shows took note of what each of them could do. That was a piece called *Mind Your Head* set on a double-decker bus, which took up all the stage. Peter Ling designed that and it was beautiful – everything on the bus worked. The bus started off from South End Green in the First Act and went to Pimlico. In the Second Act it started to come back. People got on and off the bus, bad people and good people who were exceptionally honest about their lives and occupations. You met people in the First Act and then again in the Second but something had happened to them. It did have a comic plot too. The driver was in love with his mother who was a conductress who was married to the Inspector – his uncle. The bus was called The Red Revenger and the bus driver was determined on Revenge for his father's death. So it had a highly original plot nicked from Hamlet, and a fantastic fight between the driver and the Inspector using their busman badge pins. Jonathan Pryce leapt off the top deck of the bus, killed Tony Sher who turned out to be Hitler from his dying speech. People liked it – the critics didn't.

The form of *Mind Your Head* is very similar to that of *Tyger*. The image for this kind of form is, again, a patchwork quilt. Some of the squares may be dark, some ugly, some beautiful, some gentle, one may have the Mona Lisa on, another one may portray Donald Duck, a Marie Lloyd square, a napalm square, a Hitler square etc.

That patchwork quilt is a rough metaphor for how I see society, how I see the world. I don't want to write plays about a husband and wife nagging each other to death, supported by two best friends. So my shows are mainly about public situations rather than domestic ones. I like to have as many characters as possible. I like songs, dances, fights, jumping about. I'm not interested in writing Broadway stuff (some of which I like) which has a computerised form so that the audience knows exactly where to laugh, exactly where to cry, exactly when to demand an encore.

Have you adapted from any other 'literary' works?

Man Friday was a long way out of Crusoe and *White Suit Blues* was about 70% out of Mark Twain. I don't think there's any novel that can't be done if it's good enough – in my terms. Jules Verne would be good.

I've got a feeling theatre will move further into song, dance and spectacle. Psychological realism is prevalent on the television but theatre can offer something an audience has never seen before.

When you talk of the way theatre might go I thought of *Nicholas Nickleby* at the RSC. Great, the best thing I've seen. Such emotion was going on – the audience was incredible. It wasn't sentimentality, it was naked feeling. And of course great fun.

From On Writing for Performance, *an interview*
with Peter Hulton and Alan Read in London, 1982
originally published as part of the Theatre Papers series

6. PRINCIPAL BOYS WITH NO PRINCIPLES

I love the Panto form. I remember a stage set empty except for two ladders and one plank. Enter Charlie Cairoli and company with brushes and buckets of multi-coloured whitewash. Charlie: 'Well, we've got to whitewash Prince Charming's apartment.' (End of dialogue – the next 20 minutes was all wonder-action and total hilarity.)

How They Made the Play
That Caused All the Rumpus

Beginning

It is like getting married. I've written for the theatre and about it, but never before worked in the theatre. Like getting married but the courtship is whirlwind. Sixteen days before rehearsals start I'm commissioned to take Geoffrey Skelton's admirably faithful translation of *Marat/Sade* and adapt it all into free verse, couplets, songs. Instant love for the play, but don't understand how it hangs together.

Peter Brook guides me through German text. Note the jagged rhythms and clanging rhymes of couplets, the compression of the songs, the staccato rhythm of Marat's speeches, the more sensual flow of Sade. Decide to use equivalent of rough riding couplets in English panto for rough texture of Weiss couplets. Borrow Sade books from friend of friend. A knockabout, illegal translation. Sade gives me boredom, some insight, amusement and nightmares.

Meaning

The play doesn't progress by logical steps. It jumps and the audience must jump with it.

It doesn't carry one thesis, but many meanings, some of them conflicting. This isn't only true of *Marat/Sade*. If Peter Weiss's play shoots 200-odd messages at the audience, *King Lear* must send out about 1,000. Nobody can be expected to catch them all. Nobody does.

Some themes are more important than others. The oblique debate between Marat and Sade is central. Weiss, like Marat, wants social justice. But like Sade he wants personal freedom. The socialist revolution and the sexual revolution. As Sade says in the play:

And what's the point of a revolution

Without general copulation?

Construction of the play, with other characters as puppets, means Sade must 'win' the debate with Marat. When written Weiss was on the side of both Sade's call for total individual freedom and Marat's call for revolution. But soon firmly on the side of Marat, Jacques Roux and socialism. So continually changing the end to try to make Marat win more.

Harold Hobson writes that he's not sure if he was meant to be revolted or delighted by the symbolic whipping of Sade. That's how the play operates. Most people react to the scene with mixed revulsion and delight. If they consider these reactions, try to add them up, the scene works.

The play's not only violent, it is also fiercely anti-bourgeois. When Coulmier, director of the Asylum, intervenes to say: 'I always thought that plays were meant to entertain. But how can entertainment deal in sarcasm and violence?' it was expected that some of the audience would laugh in sympathy and that the laugh would be choked off when the laughers realised they were identifying with Coulmier, the Peter Cadbury of Charenton. On the first night that's exactly what happened.

At first rehearsals the script's almost ignored; when it's looked at, it's altered. Brook announces that he has no time for traditional pretty or melodramatic stage madness. He produces books and pictures illustrating Charenton, Sade, Marat, the French Revolution. Lectures, discussions, film showings. The actors begin to improvise madness. Everyone seems to have known somebody who was mentally sick. Goya etchings of the mad are shown and used as the basis for characterisations. The production depends on this harrowing work. If one patient lapses into sanity, the world of Charenton Asylum crumbles. This exploration of madness sets the nerves on edge.

Middle

Brook works impossibly hard; everyone around him is expected to do the same. I work eighteen hours a day – at rehearsals, in the pub, at home, sometimes in my sleep. Dick Peaslee sets songs in the backroom.

Even when Brook's horribly tired he doesn't lose his temper, doesn't need to. His praise is usually given individually, privately, always at the psychologically necessary moment.

Some artists complain that he draws on the imagination of those around him. He certainly does. He likes actors with imagination. In the early weeks of *Marat/Sade* he forces actors to create their own parts, welcomes new ideas from everyone. By the fourth week most people find their creativity beginning to sag. Actors almost screaming to be told what to do. Just as morale starts to crack, Brook begins to flash out his own ideas. Like Duke Ellington, who chose wonderful individual jazz musicians and gave them their heads, writing pieces for each of them tailored to their talents and personalities and allowing them freedom to improvise. Greatness.

Betting is that the Lord Chamberlain will object to the flagellation, the Satanist Lord's Prayer and the execution of Damiens. He doesn't. Instead he censors four bits of earthy language. He ruins one song, but it could have been worse.

Later rehearsal

Assistant director Malcolm Goddard pads around showing each actor how to convert a bare stage into a Parisian market between verses of a song. Stage management busily catching up with yesterday's script cuts and additions. I'm trying to find a substitute for a limp couplet. Brook watches everything. Glenda Jackson (Charlotte Corday) is twisting, humming to herself for some happy, private reason. Clive Revill (Marat) climbs out of the tin bath in which he spends the play, to query a long speech. The new between-verses routine, designed to last three seconds, is presented. It takes five seconds. New, simplified routine worked out by Brook and Goddard, rehearsed, presented. Now it takes four seconds. That's better.

End

First-night tension extraordinary. It's like getting married – concerned friends, jocular friends, ritual, drinks. Play begins. Don't hear a word of it. Hear instead every member of the audience breathing. Try to measure the nervous content of each laugh. Interval. A gin and tonic says: 'It's so old-fashioned, all this talk about the underprivileged.' I'm wickedly delighted. The play doesn't mention the under-privileged. It talks about the poor. Second act. Tension very high. Play ends. Nerve-racked wedding reception, I mean cast party. All the men, traditionally, must kiss all the girls. Twenty men, twenty girls. Takes hours, should have been rehearsed. Brook warns me that the Press will be tough, presents me with a bottle of liqueur called Goldwasser (political joke).

Next morning. Have ordered all the papers. But who cares about critics? Unravel papers. Rave, rave, semi-rave, rave. Revelation: critics are *people*. Waves of euphoria flood London. It's like getting happily married. It's like fifty people all getting married at the same time.

Adapted version of an article originally published in
The Sunday Times *on 13 September 1964*

7. SORRY I WAS LATE

I didn't finish my first full-length show – *Tyger* – until 1971. (I'd done an apprenticeship with Peter Brook on *Marat* and *US*.) Main reason for not starting earlier in life (born 1932) was that under the bloody Lord Chamberlain the theatre couldn't deal freely with religion, sex or politics – my favourite jokes and griefs. Censorship kills. I wouldn't have finished *Tyger* without Ken Tynan. Similar help with my double-decker bus play *Mind Your Head* came from Alan Dossor of the Liverpool Everyman. Bless you, dolls.

Tynan and Tyger

It was Ken Tynan's fault. He had joined Thames TV to head an arts magazine called *Tempo*. Being Ken he dreaded working in some battery farm open-plan office in Teddington that no one important would ever visit. He demanded, and got, a penthouse suite in the Picadilly Hotel complete with a brilliant young staff, a shower and room service.

One of his lefty lieutenants, the late Clive Goodwin, must have mentioned my name as a young poet who was just about to publish a hip first novel about jazz, *If You See Me Comin'*. I was summoned to the *Tempo* suite.

I'd been excited about meeting Ken, whose work as a theatre critic I'd admired tremendously. I arrived hot from work on the *Evening Standard*, nervous as a nerve. Ken greeted me, immediately invited me to visit a mental hospital and make a film about the paintings of the patients. My personal life was such a shipwreck that a mental home loomed like Fate to me. I told him: 'I'm sorry, but I just left my wife and children today. I'd love to work for you but I'm not in a state to take on something like that.'

I heard the famous Tynan stutter for the first time. 'G-G-God,' he said. 'Sue, get them to send up a tray of martinis.' He gave me several of these anaesthetics, he waved goodbye, I thought that was it.

No. It was the beginning of a good friendship. I fell deeply in love with one of the brilliant young *Tempo* staff – we're still married thirty years later – and we became frequent, delighted guests at the Tynan house where a river of good wine flowed by and you found yourself sitting on its banks between James Cameron and James Baldwin.

Discovered by Peter Brook, I started to write for the theatre, adapting Peter Weiss's *Marat/Sade* and writing song lyrics and the odd scene for Brook's *US*. Ken meanwhile moved into a prefab office on the South Bank and started to dramaturge for the new National Theatre.

He sent for me again. I ought to write a play of my own. I told him about my dream of writing a play to celebrate the life and work of my greatest hero, William Blake. It would all be worth it to get on the English stage the supreme speech which begins:

'What is the price of Experience? Do men buy it for a song?
Or Wisdom for a dance in the street? No, it is bought with the price
Of all that a man hath, his house, his wife, his children.
Wisdom is sold in the desolate market where none come to buy,
And in the wither'd field where the farmer plows for bread in vain.'

The play would have many songs, most of them with lyrics by Blake. It would be called *Tyger*. Ken exploded. Of course I must write it. He commissioned me on the spot.

But it was my first full-length play. I was terrified of it. You write a poem or a novel and if it's a dud, only you are hurt. Write a dud play and a whole company suffers – it's an own goal at Wembley.

Living in a remote Yorkshire Dales farmhouse, I kept researching Blake and filling boxes with notes about Blake and reading books about his contemporaries and his heirs and – anything but write a scene.

Ken made his move. A brief letter arrived from the National Theatre, signed by Sir Laurence Olivier. It wondered if *Tyger* was nearly ready for the stage. It wondered politely, but with a slightly quizzical, possibly injured air. I'm a touch-typist, eight fingers two thumbs. I started playwriting as if pursued by Henry the Fifth on horseback.

It wasn't to be a biopic. It was anti-historical. Blake's enemies included Sir Joshua Rat (who stood for all commercial art) and a composite monarch called Mad King George the Fifty. Blake and his wife never had a baby, according to the official records, so I gave them one, and a lullaby about 'The Children Of Blake'. There was a birthday party for Blake, attended by Chaucer,

Shakespeare, Milton, a rock group called The Romantic Revival, Rudyard Kipling, Allen Ginsberg and a high-kicking chorus of critics who sang a verse lifted from the works of F. R. Leavis.

The show ended with Blake and his wife Kate being dispatched to the moon in a rocket, landing happily in an Ark with wings and founding the New Jerusalem. I wrote a covering letter describing it as 'a cranky panto' and sent it to Ken. Expecting rejection, I was all ready to post it on to the Royal Shakespeare Company, who had also asked me for a play.

The farmhouse phone rang. Ken. *Tyger* was wonderful. Needed some work. But they'd do it. The National. Yes. Come to London. We've got to talk about the music.

My first thought for the music had been Duke Ellington, but I knew that was impossible. The composer should be a British Ellington. I listened to all the possibles and there was one obvious choice – Mike Westbrook, who has since established himself as the greatest jazz composer in Europe. Ken wasn't sure at first. Wouldn't I be interested in John Dankworth? Of course, I said, avoiding an argument, but we'd never get him. Ken was angry, he whitened, he reached for the phone and was talking to Dankworth in seconds. He didn't commit *Tyger* to him, he was just proving something – whatever Tynan wants, Tynan gets.

Earth, air, fire and water. Dankworth was air, I thought, but I wanted the earth and fire of Westbrook. Mike appeared to us – tall, wearing battered trainers (in 1970), with the strong chin and nose and brow of – William Blake. My first impressions were correct – Mike turned out to be the most Blake-like person involved in the production.

Ken made a political move. Olivier hadn't read *Tyger*. Ken, although he didn't tell me at the time, doubted if it was really Larry's cup of tea – it was more like whisky and coke. So he waited until Sir Laurence was out of the country and then announced that the National would be putting on *Tyger* as part of its season at the New Theatre in the West End. *Fait accompli*.

At first Frank Dunlop was going to direct the play. Somehow he didn't. Suddenly both John Dexter and Michael Blakemore wanted to direct it. There were meetings. John and Michael decided to direct *Tyger* in tandem.

The band would be no problem. We would have the whole of the Mike Westbrook Band in the pit, a golden noise, the music of the New Jerusalem if ever I heard it. But what about the singing actors? The National had never done a musical.

Somehow Ken had to find out which of the actors in the company could sing. He invited them to a kind of supposedly painless audition, a party with lots of wine at which they got up, one by one, and sang a party piece. Some actors lurked, grumpily, and wouldn't perform. Many of them fell back on Gilbert and Sullivan which gave us little idea of their jazz potential. It was an embarrassing evening for everyone, but it worked.

A few actors were brought in. I had said in the script that not only the singer of the opening and closing song should be black but so should Lord Byron. (We got Isabelle Lucas and Norman Beaton). And I'd heard a very good actress singing in her dressing room in Manchester. Maureen Lipman was cast as Second Randy Woman.

I worked away at the script. I'd stuffed far too much into it – after all, I'd thought, this is my first and last play, get everything in. With Ken's help, I removed much of the stuffing. Rehearsals began. Blakemore and Dexter worked out a twin director routine. One of them would tackle the song and dance areas for two weeks, the other would work on spoken scenes. Then they'd swap over. They were always, it seemed, polite to each other, and the stormy side of Dexter, of which I'd heard frightening stories, hardly surfaced. Both directors were loyal to the play. But eyebrows were being raised already.

Olivier was back in England. The short, bloody parody of Henry the Fifth was suddenly dropped from the last act without any explanation. I didn't ask for any. The moment was not important enough to the play to warrant a showdown. I hadn't intended to hurt his feelings.

The Lord Chamberlain's censorship had finally been abolished in 1968. But in 1971 there were still taboos. One night I was invited to a party at the Oliviers' apartment. When I arrived the place seemed packed with every famous face in theatre. But no Olivier. An hour later he arrived. He walked straight across the room to me and took me by the arm and turned me and said: 'Oh, oh, Adrian. Adrian, come with me. I just want to show you something.' He led the way out of the room and down a very long corridor. What's this leading to, I wondered, a proposition? Of a kind. At the end of the corridor he stopped and stared out of a great window. There lay the Thames and beyond it towers and spires. 'Ah!' cried Olivier. Then, more deeply, disappointed: 'Oh.' 'What is it?' I asked. 'I had hoped I could have shown you the illuminated spire of a church,' he said, and smiled his sadness. 'But tonight it is not illuminated.' Sigh. 'I'd hoped to show you that spire because it is the spire of the church where my Father used to preach. And I thought, if you saw it, you might understand – that there are one or two things – one or two – in your wonderful play *Tyger* – one or two things which – worry me a little.' He laughed and took my arm. 'Come on, let's go back to the party.' This was Olivier's way of explaining to me that he didn't like me using the word clitoris in *Tyger*. 'Clitoris' had never been used on the English stage before.

Ken was on my side. We kept the clitoris. As payment we were required to have a notice in the theatre's foyer, which I deeply resented, saying: 'In the opinion of the management, *Tyger* is not, perhaps, suitable for children.' I especially despised that liberal 'perhaps' and encouraged people to take as many children to *Tyger* as possible. I don't think the clitoris hurt any of them.

Rehearsals continued. One day the entire cast were singing the slavery song which ends Act One. It becomes a chant of Blake's great slogan: For Everything that Lives is Holy – over and over again. In the rehearsal room that day the cast stood close together and kept singing that one phrase, improvising new harmonies, taking the power of the chant to new heights, looking straight into the eyes of the production team as they sang. I turned to look at Ken. He was standing with his arms crossed, full of the music, his smile total, his face scarlet, the tears running copiously down his cheeks. *Tyger* was never better.

Once again censorship threatened. Somebody had drawn Olivier's attention to an aberration in the script, and he sent for me, to the headmaster's office this time. It was about the sedition scene.

This was based on the incident when Blake was tried for sedition. A drunken soldier alleged that Blake said: 'God damn the King of England. All his soldiers are slaves, and so are all his poor people.' (Blake denied this and avoided being hanged, but it sounds like Blake all right). Olivier pointed out: 'But Adrian, in your script he says: 'God damn the Queen of England. All her soldiers are slaves and so are all her poor people.''

'Yes,' I said, 'That was on purpose. When Blake was alive it was a King, but now it's a Queen. Blake hated Kings and Warriors and – Priests too.' Olivier looked bleak. 'I see. So it's deliberate.' I said yes, Blake was an anarchist. Bless him, Olivier left it at that and never again tried to interfere with my subversive text.

Ken and I had wanted to stage *Tyger* in the Roundhouse, with great stained glass Blakes all around. In the posh New Theatre we weren't allowed even to stick a few Blake reproductions on the walls. And so a show which demands to spill out into the auditorium and then the streets was confined behind the proscenium arch.

Just before the first night I was interviewed by *Late Night Line-Up*. I was feeling high. My interviewer was a young but balding Australian, rather shy. He said he enjoyed a preview of *Tyger* and all was fine till he asked me why there were so many digressions in the play. I thought I would demonstrate the entertainment value of digressions: 'Look, ' I said, 'I'm very self-conscious about my face and body and hands, so in a public appearance like this I sometimes wear outrageous shoes so that everyone's attention will be taken by my shoes' – and I pointed at my black and white patent leather flash shoes until the camera was forced to hold them in close up – 'And all my self-consciousness runs down into my shoes and doesn't bother me at all.' I smiled, but Clive James did not smile back. Some years later he reviewed my TV play *Daft As A Brush*, placed his critical boot upon it, and ground it into the mud.

Among my first night cards I found a very cheerful erotic one from Joan Plowright, Lady Olivier. I knew she liked *Tyger* and it struck me that she might have been its guardian angel.

Tyger opened and the critics roared. Some of them loathed it, some of them loved it. Most nights some man stood up and led his family out when the word 'clitoris' was used. (In a vain rearguard attempt, Olivier had suggested it be pronounced 'cliteorice'). It was said that 'Binkie' Beaumont had walked out of the theatre on the first night white in the face muttering about 'sedition'. One critic said that the National Theatre should stick to the liberal mainstream and shouldn't be staging plays of the revolutionary left. Some of the attacks were painful – I knew I'd written an anarchist show and I should've expected it, but you think well they'll be bowled over by the beauty of Blake. Nope. If they hated the politics, and it was Blake's politics more than mine, they couldn't see.

The *Guardian* and *The Times* were enthusiastic. But the best review was in the wild underground *Oz* magazine, written by the late David Widgery. It was a love song to Blake and to *Tyger*. Unfortunately it was overprinted with purple psychedelic designs to such an extent that it was only this year that I managed, with the help of a magnifying glass, to decipher it.

The gallery was full, the stalls half-empty. The run was not extended. Ken's fierce loyalty never faltered. I was never a safe bet – but he bet on me and bet heavily. He always defended my work and our friendship lasted until his death. With *Tyger* especially he inspired me, gave me courage, set me on fire. We had many wonderful evenings together and he was the best company in the world. I miss him dreadfully – his warmth, his wit, his kindness and thoughtfulness.

But *Tyger* didn't die. It kept surfacing, especially in art schools around the world. Mike Westbrook and I did a TV version called *Glad Day* with some extra Blake songs, and Mike kept featuring the songs in his concerts

Even now people tell me that *Tyger* was the first exciting show they ever saw in the theatre. In 1993 Paines Plough, the touring theatre company and Salisbury Playhouse approached me about it.

We agreed that some of *Tyger* should be rewritten to face the nineteen-nineties. As his main artistic enemies, Blake would face not the Academic Establishment represented by Sir Joshua Rat, but the currently fashionable sadistic and necrophiliac and highly commercial art scene of 1995. The new script would also reflect great events of our time, like the Gulf War.

The National production had a cast of 33 playing 70 parts. The new version would have a company of 12-13, including the band. But one week before the show went into rehearsal, it was cancelled because of a financial crisis.

It was a sickening blow. But then I had a letter from a brilliant American ex-student of mine, Nat Warren White. He wanted to direct *Tyger Two* at Emerson College, Boston in October 1995.

And so here we are. Blake is ready to rock again. When it comes to the building of the New Jerusalem, it's just another brick in the golden wall.

Tyger was born in 1971. In 1995 it will be re-born. *Tyger Two* – just when you thought it was safe to go back into the theatre.

From Adrian's archive

Elegy for Ken Tynan

The morning after you died

my fingers wouldn't type
I switched off my typewriter
cried my way downstairs

opened the door on to the wide garden
the grass was brilliant with dew
hedgeful of birds blowing all sorts of jazz
and a brand-new sky

Fuck it!, I said,
Fuck it!

then I heard you laughing.

8. ACTORS AND POEMS
AND POETS AND POEMS

Peter O'Toole and Orson Welles can both read poetry marvellously. Because they read poetry. But very few actors and actresses make poetry part of their lives. So those anthology shows are usually grim: 'This is a poem from a woman's point of view – well you'd better do that one then Tessie'. Nobody should ever read aloud in public a poem they don't completely believe. Reading a poem calls for technique, understanding and commitment – comic and serious poems alike. Many people seem proud of their general ignorance of poetry. It's like boasting about a tin ear or colour-blindness. 'I'm afraid I'm really too busy for poetry' or 'I'm afraid I don't get enough privacy' may be true lines. But they should not be delivered with a self-congratulatory smile. But what has poetry got to do with the theatre? Shakespeare, Beckett, Arden/D'Arcy, Wilde, Brecht, Welfare State for a start. Poets worth seeing for their performances: Logue, Patten, McGough, Pete Morgan, Robert Garioch, Adrian Henri, George Barker, Ted Hughes, Heathcote Williams, Mike Horovitz, Ivor Cutler and Phyllis April King. Hello, playmates!

Imagining Jerusalem

Principles of Group Work

Mutual respect is basic. The fellow-artist whose work bores or embarrasses you now may simply be braver than you. When other group members are presenting their work, either to the group or in public, give them your total concentration. Train yourself in stillness – unless of course you're responding to the rhythm of the work.

One artist talks at a time. One discussion goes on at a time. Background muttering and whispering kills concentration.

Group work is the reverse of competition. Be glad when someone's good and show it. Be gentle with someone who's not so good, and, if you can, be helpful. We are all teachers, all students.

Whatever we hide outside the group, we should be as honest as we can within it. If we're going to travel far, trust and loyalty to each other are essential. Sincere criticism face to face can be helpful – often best offered privately rather than during a group session. Gossip about fellow members of the group, impatient put-downs etc are sabotage. Most people are afraid of most other people most of the time. But within a group like ours we should do everything we can to eliminate fear.

Don't take a proprietorial attitude to work given to the group. Work and rework it until you're ready to give it – then give it as well as you can. If it's a poem and someone wants to set it to music but would like you to rewrite it, try to cooperate. If somebody else has an idea which you can translate into a painting, a dramatic scene or anything else – use it.

Don't be afraid of seeming childish or childlike. Be as honest as you dare. I'm not much interested in length analysis of work. But interested in you having the courage to expose your work to the reaction of others – first this group – later maybe to friends, later maybe to strangers.

Groups within the Group

When we know more about each other, groups will form within the group. A poet may write a lyric, a composer may set it, several musicians may play the music, a singer may sing it, a dancer may dance it. Obviously such groups will need to meet and rehearse outside the Tuesday meeting.

Look out for other people to work with. An artist and a playwright may combine to produce a poster or comic book. Don't be afraid to break down categories. If you're a poet, try to sing, dance, play an instrument, paint.

We want to communicate as many visions as possible. Not just one from each member of the group. So try to work with several different groups within the group.

Visions

To paraphrase William Blake – everyone has the power to see visions, but they lose it because they don't work on it. Everyone has daydreams. Work on your daydreams. Concentrate on the images you see in them. Return to those images. Discard the ones which seem useless. The next stage is to try to translate those images into some form which will communicate – songs, sculpture, paintings, maps, models, jokes, dramatic scenes, dance, happenings, costumes – but see the vision first and see it in as much detail as possible. Don't worry about how small the vision may seem – one line of poetry, one bar of music. Don't worry about how far out or absurd. Nothing is far out in this project. And visions needn't be solemn. Third stage is to try to communicate your vision to other people through your art and especially through your combined arts.

Reasons for the Project

* The creation of the group itself. It's an exercise in working cooperatively with artists from different disciplines. It's a one-semester group, but the hope is that it may help you to form your own creative groups in future.

* Second point is the creation of a show depicting details of the societies in which we'd like to live, however conflicting. Will be good if we can also include the visions of people around us, university or town, or school. We'll decide together what form the show will take, where it will be performed etc. We may decide to give the show for friends only. Or to anyone who wants it.

* If we drive our imaginations hard enough to see and communicate some details of the lives we'd like to live, the harder we'll work towards our own New Jerusalems.

Details of Jerusalem

Concentrate on detail rather than social theory. Images rather than rhetoric. If you wanted to show what crime would be like in Utopia Jerusalem – give us a court scene. Make lists of elements in society and try to see how you'd like them to be – science, education, transport, finance, art, family life, sport, music, mass media, animals, psychiatry, religion, dance, race relations, treatment of children, architecture, humour, food – and who does the dirty work – mines, garbage. What about security? Internal and external? What sort of housing? Small things or large things. Design a sidewalk, each paving stone different, if you like the idea. Invent. A new sport – special equipment enables people to walk along the tops of clouds – cloud-climbing. Nothing, I repeat, is far out.

We haven't got the time to worry about how these things can be achieved. See a city square – would there be statues? If so, statues of what? Would they move and make music? What would your job or jobs be?

...

Tasks

<u>Continuous</u> Bring some work towards the final project every week, however rough, however brief. A list of good images is better than a vague essay.

<u>This week</u> Design and make an LP sleeve. The imaginary disc inside is a record of your life from now on – as you would like it to go, as you'd like to live it. Front of sleeve should have title, your name and a photo of you. Use collage, water-colours, any technique. Make sleeve so that it can fold out so back and front visible at once. Back should have two columns of liner

notes. One giving hard facts about any skills you have, singing, dancing, composing, instruments played – also carpentry, dressmaking, cooking, fire-eating. Second column, written in third person – an account of your life from the end of this semester until your death. A happy life and a happy death, with everything achieved you want. Please type liner notes, and everything else if possible.

LP sleeves are for the benefit of all the group. So we can get to know each other quickly. Facts from the sleeves will soon be incorporated into a fact sheet for all group members – facts about your skill and experience, that is.

Delivered as part of Adrian's 'Imagining Jerusalem'
course at Wesleyan University, 1973

9. GIMLET, PRINCE OF DENMARK

Hamlet is often on my mind. Almost everybody would like to play the part. I believe there ought to be a National Without The Prince Theatre in which 365 days a year there would be a production of Hamlet with a different Prince, chosen by lot, every night. Cast would respond to the lead interpretation. I'll do my stint. The best Hamlet I ever saw was David Warner. Hamlet's a devil with the gag. I'd like to see Sylvester McCoy do it. But the next definitive version's likely to come from Jonathan Pryce. I used to write for him when he was on at the Liverpool Everyman and it's lovely to sit round the fridge on long winter evenings and reminisce about the good old days in Hope Street. I interviewed the Beatles twice. Now you drop a name.

Theatre in the Wild

I've spent tens of thousands of hours sitting in theatres, and mostly I could have had a more exciting time in my own dreams. But the Everyman, when I first climbed aboard her in 1972, was a stormy ship with the skull and crossbones nailed to the mast. First show I saw there was a Brecht, re-set in a Liverpool building site. The builders were on strike and on to the stage came a university student, offering to entertain the men with his drama group. The student was extraordinary, lean, dark, angular, with a voice like Lester Young's tenor sax sometimes, like Cootie Williams' trumpet sometimes, he could sing, he could move, he could act in a way that made you sit up and say, hey, this could be a great actor on the prowl. It was Jonathan Pryce, former Butlins redcoat, and on the way to being the greatest actor of his time. But he was a star in a company of stars – there were about twelve in the regular company run by Alan Dossor for the Everyman at the time, so you could do a funky Shakespeare if you had to. Alan asked me to write a show for the company, which my wife Celia Hewitt was acting in, and so I watched them night after night and wrote *Mind Your Head*, a nutty story set on a

London double-decker bus, creating parts for Jonathan, for Celia, for Antony Sher, for Bernard Hill and Philip Joseph and Angela Phillips and Richard Williams and sweet Bob Putt. It was a great way to work and to make a story for the stage. It was hard work and fun work with a wonderful gang of fantastically talented lefty nutters. The further out the story, the better they liked it. Alan Dossor was a driven and wonderful director.

Peter Ling and his design team were just as fanatical. They wheeled a real double-decker out of the local bus garage, had it cut in half so the audience could see inside, managed to articulate it so that the driver's cab was turning round a corner and the conductress's platform was swinging along behind. We never thought it'd be finished in time. But they stayed up all night and next morning led us in to show us the magic bus, now painted a brilliant London red, filling the entire stage. And they sat us down and showed us how every light and headlight and bell and buzzer and horn on that bus worked. I've never had a happier, wilder time working in the theatre, in the bar, in the streets of a city I'd come to first a few years earlier when my dear friends Roger McGough, Brian Patten and Adrian Henri introduced me to Liverpool, my adventure playground and my sweetheart of cities. Since then I've come back to the Everyman whenever I could, most recently to read poems with Paul McCartney, Willy Russell and others to celebrate Adrian Henri's life, and for Gemma Bodinetz's brilliant revival of my version of *The Mayar of Zalamea*. Happy 40th birthday, Everyman, sail on, sail on over the ocean of dreams.

love and peace from
Adrian Mitchell (Ancient Mariner)

Written on the occasion of the
Liverpool Everyman's 40th Anniversary in 2004

10. WHY I TURNED DOWN A KNIGHTHOOD

Within the Revolution every style is possible except Socialist Realism. Socialist Realism sells the people short. It denies the eloquence, wit, poetry and imagination of the people. It denies that they can sing and dance and love. It affirms only a kind of glum solidarity that moves in gumboots.

John Fox and Welfare State International

Once upon 1968, I found myself in a Lancaster park swinging a baby alarm loudspeaker round my head and chanting into its microphone William Blake's *Proverbs of Hell.* 'Enough – or Too Much!' and 'The Road of Excess leads to the Palace of Wisdom' were two of the holy slogans. Trying hard to look avant-garde, I was taking part in Welfare State International's very first gig – *The Marriage of Heaven and Hell.*

1968 was the year when the Angel Bohemia spread her fiery wings. I was chanting for Blake's sake, but also because I was fascinated by the artists, musicians and poets who were creating Welfare State International (WSI) – which later became my favourite theatre group in the world.

WSI has always been made up of extraordinary people creating imaginary palaces for everybody even when wet, cold, soaked, hungry, mocked and insulted by some of the most mudheaded Hooligan Heritage Committees and Aesthetic Bureaucrats in the land. Brave people with big eyes. Many visionary shows, both great and small, were generated as these extraordinary people worked together – hairy folkies, keen-eared electronic wizards, firework spacewalkers, dragon painters, stegosaurus actors, patient stone-carvers, galloping one-man-bands, acrobatic poets and prophets in all sizes – a great deal of love giving birth to tiny and gigantic images of flame.

I never ran away to join this circus – I had too many people to support financially. But I wrote for them when I could and ran workshops and sometimes sent new recruits, two of my daughters included. What sort of people did WSI need? Years ago I was running a project at Dartington College of the Arts – a Mud Fair. On the floor, making a costume for himself, sat one of the best students I ever met in my life. As a boy he had taught himself stage magic. He could sing, act, play any instrument you could name – and he looked at the world through big round innocent eyes. I was worrying about some big props we needed for the Fair and asked him, 'You know we need some ten-foot-high sticks with ghosts at the top we can swing around over the heads of the audience? Well, how many of our group do you think can make them?' My student looked at me in surprise. 'Oh I think we all can', he said, teaching me one of the greatest lessons of my life. His name was Andy Burton and he went on to be one of the State's finest creators and then went further on to found, with his wife Jill, a shining and surviving small travelling company called The Satellites. It's a joy to work with people like that and John Fox pays tribute to them.

Much of the finest design in indoor theatres has been inspired by WSI – Peter Brook's *Mahabharata* at the Tramshed in Glasgow, with rose-red brickwork half as old as time and the ever-changing colours and shadows of its puddle-lake; the working costumes of Julie Taymor's *The Lion King*, so glorious they made you weep; the secret drawers and sudden revelations of *Shockheaded Peter*. All these were wonderful and all of them were influenced by the bravado and poetry of WSI designs.

Foxy himself is a poet, painter and maker with enormous imaginative energy. A phone call to him is like a bumpy magic-carpet ride, the ideas and images are torrential. I usually hang up determined to accomplish Seven Impossible Tasks before breakfast. *Eyes on Stalks*, which must be read alongside the very practical and inspiring *Engineers of the Imagination*, is an account of a personal journey as one of the chieftains of the WSI tribe. It's full of stories – exhilarating accounts of gigs in Australia and Japan and the raising of the Titanic in London docks, clashes, with arrogant cultural bureaucrats and delicate descriptions of naming ceremonies.

Now, it seems, John and the company have settled down in their purpose-built palace in Ulverston, birthplace of the great Stan Laurel. Maybe the Road of Excess led them to the Palace of Wisdom. But I don't think that road's seen the last of them.

Adapted foreword to John Fox, Eyes on Stalks *published in 2002*

11. TO BE CARVED OVER THE ENTRANCE
TO THE NATIONAL THEATRE

There's one good thing about a cow-pat:
If you leave it in the sun it dries.
And there's one good thing about Capitalism –

It dies.

John McGrath

Socialism is alive. Theatre is alive. Socialist theatre is alive. And, in every sense except the literal one, John McGrath, whose body gave up a long, brave fight against illness in January this year, is alive and kicking – Liberal and Tory arses for choice.

I first met John when he was a lanky undergraduate at Oxford when I interviewed him for the local paper. One of his first plays, *A Man Has Two Fathers*, was being staged and he'd just written his first radio play, *The Tent*. We argued a bit and laughed a lot and the fire of his writing and his character warmed my heart.

We have been friends and comrades ever since. He also became one of his heroes and he always will be. I shall never forget my visits to John and his beloved wife Liz – the actress Elizabeth MacLennan – at their flat in Edinburgh and later at the Royal Marsden Hospital.

They gave me lessons in love and courage.

I think of John with the wind in his wild hair, even indoors. He was a man born for adventures, with his crackling humour and those soulful eyes and that strong deep heart and that fighting mind. Robert Louis Stevenson would have loved John, and put him in his novels. He'd have been great in *Kidnapped* or *Treasure Island*. Stevenson loved to write about friendship, and friendship was one of John's greatest gifts.

Speaking through essays, talks, letters and poems, this new book of John's records many of his triumphs and his failures too. Of course he wasn't just a playwright and a poet – that wouldn't have been enough for such a passionate, all-or-nothing highwayman.

He had to found his own theatre companies – 7:84 in England and Scotland (7:84 to ram home the fact that seven per cent of the people in Britain own 84 per cent of its wealth). And of course that led to trouble – it's tough enough to write plays, but to direct them as well and try to organise troupes of actors and musicians on tours to the remotest (and most beautiful) corners of Britain is a task for a trio like Superman, Lenin and Duke Ellington.

That he succeeded so often and so triumphantly, on stage and television, despite cultural bureaucrats who suspected him, rightly, of preaching an enjoyable revolution, is partly because of his strong convictions and will and imagination, but also very much because of the talents and the total loyalty of his wonderful family.

Of course John's work did not spring out of nothing – he worked in a tradition, but a tradition which was a mixture of *The Beggar's Opera*, Brecht and, above all, Joan Littlewood and Gerry Raffles' Theatre Workshop. And John's work will not fade into nothing – there are so many artists in theatre, TV and movies who have learned from his work – lessons in vision and courage and imagination.

Last Sunday I travelled to Edinburgh for *A Good Night Out*, a celebration of John's life at the Assembly Rooms. There must have been at least 700 people packed in, almost all of whom knew or worked with John at some stage – musicians and singers of all kinds, actors of all ages, singers and dancers and poets. It was a four-hour extravaganza of John's work for stage and film devised by his wife Liz and produced by his daughter Kate. A patchwork of songs, scenes from plays, poems, film clips it was a glorious celebration, full of laughter and tears, culminating in a ceilidh.

Even when he was confined to his bed, in the last months, John worked. In the last weeks he was completing *HyperLynx*, a tough and highly topical play he wrote for Liz to act. I have seen the first act, and it is one of his most powerful, urgent and humane works. And John's *Eight Plays For England* is published soon by Exeter University Press.

Read *Naked Thoughts*.[3] If you're interested in the future of the theatre or the future of the human race, it will inspire you. And if your interests lie more in how to make the maximum profit out of the people around you and how to keep the poor and helpless of the world in their place, this book will kick your arse.

John McGrath is one of the visionaries without whom there is no progress. He turned his back on the doubters and the snobs and made wonderful theatre for the people. Read his book, see his plays and rise to the challenges he laid down. Thank you, John, for everything.

Originally published in Camden New Journal, *2002*

---

3   John McGrath, *Naked Thoughts That Roam About: Reflections on Theatre*, edited by Nadine Holdsworth

12. BLACK QUOTA

Very few people seem awake to the widespread and everyday discrimination against non-white actors. Obviously there are some plays where colour is relevant to the meaning of the play – when the subject is slavery, colonialism, prejudice, etc. And in realistic plays. But audiences are far more imaginative than they're usually allowed to be. Who cares if King Lear is black, one of his daughters golden, one brown and one pink? Or if the Three Sisters are cast purely for ability with no consideration given to colour? One way through with new plays: in *Tyger* I wrote specifically the direction that Lord Byron was black. I got Norman Beaton – smashing. But nobody ever questioned *why* Lord Byron was black. It's easy to do. Instead of *(Enter a motor-cyclist)* write *(Enter a black motor-cyclist)*. Fill the quota, doll.

Theatre and the Left

I'd like to re-cap some recent history, because I believe that in the past 25 years there have been two major victories for a free and popular theatre in Britain.

The first major victory came in the mid-1950s with the creation of a battling political theatre by Joan Littlewood and Gerry Raffles at Theatre Workshop. Shows like *The Hostage*, *A Taste of Honey* and *Oh! What a Lovely War* opened up new roads which we're still exploring. At the same time the Royal Court was mounting plays like *Endgame*, *Serjeant Musgrave's Dance* and *Roots* – all of which asked new and vital questions without supplying glib answers. (Of course there were other political theatres at the time – Unity and the Traverse for instance.)

But the most likely medium for the left-wing writer in the mid-fifties and early sixties was still the novel, poetry or TV. Because, under the censorship of the Lord Chamberlain, the most serious contemporary aspects of religion, sex and politics couldn't be represented, discussed or commented on by what Howard Schuman calls The Show Business.

It was after a centuries-old battle in which many artists fought that official stage censorship was abolished in 1968. I remind you of these two battles as examples of the ways in which the people's will can win.

Even before the abolition of official censorship, the Cartoon Archetypical Slogan Theatre had been stomping the country for socialism. They were then joined by 7:84. And with other groups – like Welfare State and the People Show – high standards of skill and imagination were established. All these groups began and survived, thanks to the ingenuity and self-sacrifice of their members, without grants.

Apart from the flourishing of touring groups, the other major result of the abolition of official censorship has been the establishment of fringe theatre, especially in London. Back in 1965 there was virtually No Fringe Theatre at all, and I remind you of this as one of the ruins that Gaitskell knocked about a bit.

The real point of all this history is to show you how far the cultural revolution has leaped in the past 25 years. We've still got a long way to go, of course, but we'd better defend each other in the meantime from all reactionaries who want to impose censorship of any kind.

We should send a message to the Arts Council and to all regional arts councils protesting against the attempts to stop North West Spanner's grant. We should also applaud Roy Shaw [Secretary-General of the Arts Council of Great Britain] for his statement: 'The Arts Council makes no political judgments, only artistic ones, and it would deplore the introduction in the world of the arts of any form of political discrimination.'

Absolutely. The people themselves must be left to discriminate politically. And of course bad artists shouldn't get grants for being good socialists. Because bad theatre which calls itself socialist is destructive – it makes even the revolution seem boring. There's some talk of how would we deal with a National Front theatre group? The same way we deal with the National Front. By demonstration where necessary, by mockery, and by the Race Relations Act.

If the Tories are returned at the next election, things will get much tougher, and I think most of us can expect to have our grants reduced or taken away altogether. We have to fight that, but even if we lost temporarily, it's not the end of the world.

Fidel Castro said: And then you hear a revolutionary say: They crushed us! They organised 200 radio programmes, so many newspapers, so many magazines, so many TV shows, so many of this and so many of that. And one wants to ask him: What did you expect? That they would put TV, radio, the magazines, the newspapers, the printing shops – all this at your disposal? Or are you unaware that these are the instruments of the ruling class designed explicitly for crushing the Revolution? Unquote. Better to be amateurs for the revolution than pimps for a dead culture. And the revolution – which is a continuous process, not a bloodbath followed by a rigid system based on fear and dogma – needs as many visions, imaginations, ideas, people as are willing to work for it.

For a long time the theatre in this country was, with a few exceptions in each decade, the instrument of the ruling class. Much of the theatre still is precisely that. Glyndebourne, Chichester, Stratford-upon-Avon and Windsor are all political theatres. Of the Right. But today the Left has in its hands most of the vital theatre in this country. We have our own disagreements and it's right that we should argue them out. But it's essential that we should unite every time a group like North West Spanner is threatened by Tories who would like to kill every vestige of life on the theatrical Left.

From a letter to the theatre group North West Spanner after a Conservative councillor attempted to cut their funding in 1977.

13. A BEANO VISION OF THE REVOLUTION IN THE YOUNG VIC

I was pacing a dressing room in the Young Vic when a Vision cameth unto me. At first it was sound only and it spake and did say: 'The Revolution has already started and it will continue forever because a new society will develop which will constantly change in response to the changes in the People, as a lover responds to a lover. But one thing which most people have missed is that the Revolution will be extremely *funny*, the Number One Joke, the Custard Pie in the face of all Systems'…

Then the vision came on in my Vision. I saw four cartoon frames in the style of Dennis the Menace in the Beano:

Frame One: Capitalism striding down the boulevard, top hat, gold-waistcoated stomach, the school bully grown scarlet-faced, crunching the skulls of which the pavement is composed.

Frame Two: The new bully which passes under the false name of Soviet Communism striding down the same pavement in the opposite direction.

Frame Three: Capitalism and Soviet Communism both step on the same banana skin simultaneously, bump heads and see stars (and about time too).

Frame Four: A disreputable figure, alias the People, skids off round the corner on roller skates eating a skinless banana.

The Making of a Just William Play

'Y'know…I think it's time there was another rebellion in England. It's 1926 now, and we haven't had a really good rebellion since – well, the ones in hist'ry. I mean, when people put the days we're livin' in now into the hist'ry books in a hundred years' time, England's goin' to look jolly dull without a few rebellions. But there don't seem to be any rebels left – 'cept me and the Outlaws.

An' Jumble.'

That's the opening speech of my William play.

Let me take you back now to the late summer of 1939. We opened a door in the green train for London and climbed into a third-class carriage – my mother, my elder brother Jimmy and me.

It was the end of a seaside holiday in Devon – red earth, yellow sands, scones with strawberry jam crowned with cream. I settled into a corner and scanned passing passengers with my fine new telescope.

There was a loud crackle outside – then a giant voice: 'Evacuees will be arriving tonight. Evacuees will be arriving tonight.'

My Mother jumped. 'Quick, boys! Out we go.' She had suddenly decided to evacuate herself and us – so quickly that I left my beloved telescope on the train. We were soon established in a Somerset farmhouse.

My Father, who'd been in the First War, stayed in London as a government scientist, writing us wonderfully daft letters about the adventures of Felix the Cat. My Mother read to us every night – *Treasure Island*, *The Wind in the Willows*, *Just William*.

In the deep midwinter I fell ill. I was seven. Simultaneously I had measles, earache and toothache. They all reached a climax one icy January midnight. My fever raged. My Mother found the only way to calm me was by reading aloud.

The first story she read me, in my delirium, was *All the News* from *William in Trouble*. That's the one in which William and the Outlaws decide to start a newspaper. Violet Elizabeth's contribution is a crothword – with two words of three letters each. The clues are –'1 down – Wot you hav drops of. 1 across – Opposit of cat.'

'William looked at this sternly for a long time.

"Well, what is it?" he said at last.

"Can't you gueth it, William," said Violet Elizabeth.

"ith cough an' dog. C-O-F – Cough."'

I giggled, then cackled, then guffawed.

My Mother had to read it again. And again. And again. By the end of the night my pains were gone and my fate was sealed.

By the time I was nine I was a rebel. I cultivated hair which stood up at the back. If my socks ever stayed up, I rolled 'em down.

I collected mud and managed to obtain a cross between a cocker spaniel and a black retriever. He was my loving shadow and I named him Jumble.

Thus I modelled my life on William Brown (and also William Blake). They made me what I am today. Like William in *All the News*, I had a brief but bumpy career as a newspaperman.

But as soon as I could, I ran away to join the theatre – writing plays of all kinds and adapting foreign classics. Most of my plays have been celebrations of my artistic heroes – including Mark Twain, William Blake, Erik Satie, Hoagy Carmichael, Bix Beiderbecke and Beatrix Potter. And I always wanted to celebrate William.

Onwards. By the time we reached the Seventies the *Guardian* had written an article about my work headlined: THE NAUGHTY BOY OF ENGLISH LETTERS. It's true – as I paddle my leaky canoe through the Henley Regatta of English Literature I often feel like Just William at a Jane Austen tea-party.

Cut to 1984. I was working with Peter Hall at the National on a production of *Animal Farm* for which I wrote the lyrics of 28 songs, 26 of which were used. To understand Peter, I read his memoirs and discovered that he used to read William books on his daily train rides to and from school. After asking if he had seen a fine new telescope, I asked him why we didn't do a Just William play together.

Done. Peter commissioned *Just William or England in Trouble*. Basically this would be a series of scenes with William and the Outlaws from the Nineteen Twenties up to the present day. England, its scenery and its adults, would change. But William and the Outlaws would remain constant – accident-prone rebels against injustice.

One problem: the huge number of characters needed for a series of stories. (At my last count – 28 of them.) Peter proposed to solve this by having the grown-ups in masks, the children without masks. All parts would be played by adults for reasons of skill and stamina. (Except Jumble.)

Writing this epic was a grand excuse for me to buy a complete library of William books. It took a few years to hunt them all down, but I managed with the help of Highgate's glorious second-hand bookshop – *Ripping Yarns*. (Which, happily, is run by my wife, the actress Celia Hewitt.) Now all our William books stand in a locked, glass-fronted bookcase guarded by our Golden Retriever, Daisy the Dog of Peace.

Progress report. I delivered the first draft to Peter

late in 1984. The second draft, after consultation, early in 1985. Nicholas Wright the playwright, then the National Theatre's Literary Manager, was asked to read the play by Peter. His contribution was the thought that the story of William and the Nasties should be in the play to reflect the nineteen thirties. Peter thought so too. I didn't. I always found the Outlaws' Jew-baiting of a sweetshop manager painful, especially in post-Holocaust years. But I tried, reluctantly, to tackle the scene.

Early in the Nineties there was a reading of the script at Peter's house. We had fine actors. Miriam Margolyes was Violet Elizabeth Bott. And our William was Paul Merton. They sounded great. Paul wasn't happy with the Nasties scene. Nor me. Peter changed his mind. I wrote another draft, removing the Nasties with some relief. The centuries rolled on.

Peter kept trying to get the play staged. But his producers changed. The hardest-working man in show business – apart from James Brown – Peter was working all over the world, directing plays and operas, sometimes simultaneously.

Peter has always been one of my favourite directors, not only for his mastery of the stage but for the fact that whenever I submit a script to him he reads it and replies – usually positively – within seven days! He remains firm that the show will go on. I believe him.

Now one of the best things about this long and frustrating process has been corresponding with and meeting Richmal Ashbee. From the start she responded to my script and my queries with patience and kindly good humour. She made several suggestions, all of which I adopted. She was especially helpful in her comments on a scene in which Richmal Crompton meets William and the Outlaws. When I went to visit her and her husband Paul in Norfolk, they were both very welcoming. Richmal was funny and wise and warm – very like the Richmal Crompton I have always imagined. I really value her helpful letters.

I don't want to reveal too much about the play what I wrote. But it kicks off with my favourite story, *All the News*. The characters include William, the Outlaws, the Brown and Bott families, various village children, Uncle Frederick, Richmal Crompton, Winston Churchill and Jumble.

The play's based, mostly, on a series of William stories, but some of them have been mixed together. It would be hard now to name all the stories from which I've used plotlines or speeches. But these are the titles of the scenes in *Just William or England in Trouble*.

Act One: The Twenties.

Act Two: The Thirties.

Act Three: Wartime.

Act Four: Post-War. William Forever.

I would like to finish with the final speech of the play, spoken by William to the Outlaws.

'Y'know…I think it's time there was another rebellion in England. It's 2006 now, and we haven't had a really good rebellion since – well, the ones in hist'ry. I mean, when people put the days we're livin' in now into the hist'ry books in a hundred years time, England's goin' to look jolly dull without a few rebellions. But there don't seem to be many rebels left. *(WILLIAM nods to the audience).* C'mon Jumble.'

From Adrian's archive

14. GREAT GLORY

Some of the greatest moments of glory I have known in the theatre/concert hall.
Paul Robeson singing to the full Albert Hall
Gielgud's King Lear and Paul Muni's Willy Loman
Ken Campbell's *School for Clowns*
Allen Ginsberg reading Blake and Ginsberg at the Roundhouse.

The Most Important Audience

Every town which now supports a theatre for adults should have a children's theatre – open all year round.

Theatre for children

Theatres should stage their own plays, shows, concerts and other events for children and play hosts to good touring companies and artists. They should also tour their own work.

It is essential to bring in the primary school audience, often seeing a real live play or a musician playing an instrument for the first time. These visits should be paid for as a necessary part of a child's education – not as an optional extra. Paid for by the government. All right, by all of us, as part of our taxes.

Theatre by children

Through clubs, workshops and visits to schools, the children's theatre should help develop plays, shows, concerts and other events by children – to be rehearsed and staged primarily for other children.

Continuity

It's very hard for any kind of theatre to develop without a company. Much of the best theatre work I've seen has been by companies in which actors, directors, composers, choreographers etc have worked together over several years. The classic example is the Berliner Ensemble. But I'd also cite the work of Joan Littlewood with Theatre Workshop, of Peter Brook in London and Paris, of Peter Hall and John Barton at the Royal Shakespeare Company, Alan Dossor at the Liverpool Everyman, Richard Eyre at the Nottingham Playhouse and a succession of brilliant company leaders at the Unicorn Theatre for Children.

Any company offering original work by and for children needs not only an Artistic Director and a Business Manager and a Musical Director but also a Dramaturge who will write and commission plays of all kinds by children and adults and, where necessary, advise new writers and the performers who want to devise their own shows.

Only the best

Our literature has many of the finest writers for children – Edith Nesbit, Beatrix Potter, Edward Lear, Lewis Carroll, Leon Garfield, Susan Cooper and many others.

We want to tempt our best playwrights and poets and novelists to write plays and shows for children. The best time to catch them is when they have young children of their own.

We also want to tempt the best theatre artists of all kinds into working with and for children. Once they've tried it, most of them will be so exhilarated by an audience with wide-open minds and imaginations that they'll be hooked for life.

We must insist on the highest standards for such theatre and not be afraid to criticise when shoddy or uninspired work is staged.

Adrian Noble made a great speech to the troops before we started the first rehearsals of *The Lion, the Witch and the Wardrobe*. The most important thing he said was that the story was like a Shakespeare history play, and he would direct it as seriously as that, a chronicle play out of the history of Narnia. And he did.

The care and feeding of young artists

Every child should have the chance to become an artist.

The basic necessities:

Love, warmth and respect at home.

Decent food, we still have undernourished kids in Britain.

The company of animals.

Privacy when they want it. Ideally a room each.

Easy access to book, record and tape libraries.

Enjoyment of both town and country.

Protection from mental and physical violence at home, in the streets and at school.

Time and scope at school to enjoy and practice the creative arts.

Freedom from constant testing and examinations.

A maximum class size of 15. An average class size of 12. Even Jesus couldn't manage more than 12.

Visits to theatres, museum, concert halls, galleries and exciting places of all kinds.

Most of these things are easily available to the child of well-off parents with artistic sympathies. That's why most of our professional artists come from middle-class families. But the arts are not luxuries, but necessities. The arts feed the imagination and the soul. They are for everybody. They must be open to everybody.

Audience training

Audiences are not born but made.

From three onwards there should be something at the theatre for them to enjoy. Later act Shakespeare scenes with them and prepare them before you take them to a Shakespeare production.

So they can see how great it is. So they can understand how deep it is. So they can know how hard it is.

My personal trainers

I was read to every night of my life from the age of about six months by my mother and father. Beatrix Potter, *The Wind in the Willows*, *Treasure Island*. (I was lucky, middle-class, with loving parents who enjoyed books.)

The first play I went to was *Bucky's Bears*. I was three and a half. There were three polar bears – Father Bear, Mother Bear and Baby Bear. They lived together on an iceberg. One day the Baby Bear swallowed a bar of soap. He blew out bubbles. Really they were balloons. I laughed so much I fell off my seat. I have never been happier.

(Nowadays I put animals in my plays whenever possible. I put a polar bear in *The Snow Queen*. And last year in the Dream Factory outside Warwick, a wonderful new space for youth theatre, I had a play staged with an iceberg. The iceberg melted and a Mammoth stepped out. The Mammoth was called Daisy. But I digress.)

At nine I was told to write an essay called 'The Animals' Brain Trust'. I wrote a play instead.

My teacher, a great man called Michael Bell, read my play, frowned and sent me off to do the shopping for the school. When I came back the other boys and Mr Bell acted my play. And at the end of term we put it on again with me in the part of Commander Kangaroo. I fought a duel with Professor Toad. My parents and my brother were in an audience which laughed and clapped. I was hooked.

Theatre to me has been one of my main ways of understanding the world. Chekhov and Gogol have taught me more about Russia than all the history books I've plodded through. Shakespeare has taught me more about the human spirit than any other person outside my family. But to understand theatre you have to experience theatre and the more the better and the earlier the better.

Horror of kids in theatres

When *The Pied Piper* was first proposed at the National with about sixty kids from assorted London schools playing the parts of suicidal rats and runaway children, some of the theatre staff were terrified of a backstage full of brattish screaming and vandalism. But the kids were far less trouble than trained and supposedly grown-up actors. They never got drunk for a start. And they never –

We had one fight, for which we handed out a couple of yellow cards, and otherwise – peace and glory.

Horror of teenagers in theatres

Once a year the papers print a story about Teenagers misbehaving during a theatre visit. About 200 O-level students are led into the 1,000 seater Gormenghast Empire. Only ten of them have been to the theatre before and that was to see Bonnie Langford in *Humpty Dumpty*. The play is always Shakespeare and invariably *Macbeth*.

Lady Macbeth
In the saloon bar afterwards

It was all going surprisingly well -
Our first school matinee and we'd got up to
My sleepwalking scene with the minimum of titters.
Right, enter me, somnambulistically.
One deep sigh. Then some lout tosses
A banana on to the forestage.
It got a round? Darling, it got a thunderstorm!
Of course, we carried on, but suddenly
We had a panto audience
Yelling out: 'Look out! He's behind you!'
Murders, battles, Birnham Wood, great poetry –
All reduced to mockery.
The Bard upstaged by a banana.
Afterwards we had a flaming row in the Grenville
About just who should have removed it

And just when –
One of the servants, obviously.
And ever since, at every performance:
Enter myself in those exquisite ribbons
And – plomp –- a new out-front banana.
Well, yes it does affect all our performances
But actually they seem to love it.
And how, now Ben's in Canada
Doling out Wesker to the Eskimos,
Can we decide who exits with Banana?
You can't expect me to parade down there,
Do a sort of boob-baring curtsey and announce:
'Is this a banana that I see before me?'
Anyway, darling, we may have egg on our faces -
But we've got a hit on our hands.

Too late, too late, much too late...

The most important audience

Look around you at the National during the middle of a run of a successful play, or at the Barbican. Mostly people whose character and values are formed and in many cases set like concrete. They know what a play is, they know what a musical is, they know what the bloody universe is. So nothing much is happening.

Now go to the Unicorn or the Polka theatre on a term-time weekday.

An auditorium full of kids from primary school. They are busily thinking and reacting to the building, to the seats, to each other, to the ushers, to the stage. Sometimes most of them have never been to the theatre before. The lights go down, which always silences an adult audience. But when the lights go down on this lot, they cheer. They're the most wide-open of audiences. Their concentration is intense, but it doesn't last too long if nothing new happens on stage. If they're bored, they'll turn and talk to each other. If it's a good show the stillness and focus of the audience can be uncanny. The production team sit at the back and watch for restlessness. This is an open audience in its reactions. You can tell where the play needs fixing. So you fix it, before the next performance if possible.

Plays and shows and concerts can present children with visions, ideas, challenges, wonder, sadness and joy. A good production can open so many doors that lives are changed, that young minds get a real taste of the freedom the arts can bring. A good production for children may change many lives.

Of course we want to build an audience for the future. But more importantly we want to build the actors, singers, musicians, writers, directors, designers, dancers, stagehands of the future. This is the most important audience in the world.

They are the most important audience if we show them some vision of beauty. So that they know they can see visions. They will keep that vision all their life. If we disgust them or wound them or intimidate them or make them feel stupid, then we harm them and deform their lives.

The most important
member of an audience

Some years ago I wrote Beatrix Potter's *Tom Kitten and His Friends* for the Unicorn Theatre. It was my first play for three to five year olds. My granddaughter Caitlin was three and a half. It was her first theatre. She sat still and silent throughout both halves, not laughing or clapping, just watching. She was silent on the bus home.

But as soon as we were home, Caitlin lined up all the available adults, told them their parts, cast herself as Tom Kitten and starred and directed in a wonderful production, knowing all the songs by heart.

I'm hooked and so is she. When she was nearly five my wife and I her took her to a walkabout version of *Alice in Wonderland* by the London Bubble Theatre Company. It was a superb production, but as it grew dark and the White Rabbit guided us with a flaming torch, we wondered if Caitlin wasn't too tired to stay to the end. But before we could speak she turned to us and said, 'I'd like to stay here for ever.' We stayed, and shared her delight.

When she was five and a half she took me to *Guys and Dolls* at the National, and we were both in Heaven. Since then we've taken her and her little sister Zoe to many productions, including my versions of *The Lion, the Witch and the Wardrobe* and *Jemima Puddleduck and Her Friends*. Nowadays Caitlin laughs and claps and is just about my ideal audience.

So when I'm writing for children of about eight, which is maybe my favourite age, I don't think I am Writing For Children. No, I'm Writing for Caitlin. There are millions of kids like Caitlin – the most important audience. Every one of these kids has the right to the joy that the theatre and the other arts can bring. We must make sure they are given that joy.

From Adrian's archive

15. ATTITUDE TO AUDIENCE

That's the basic one – for poetry readings or shows. My attitude is this: I assume the audience is composed of my friends and allies or people who would be my friends and allies if we knew each other better. I'll make my friends jump out of their skins on occasions, but only for a good reason. I can tell my friends terrible facts, strange stories, do tricks, sing songs, anything at all, if my attitude's right. (Of course there may be potential or actual enemies in the audience. Don't worry about them. Have an early interval so they can leave.)

For the Cast of
The Lion, the Witch and the Wardrobe

A call on the eve of battle…

Thank you all for your patience and your wonderful work.

You are a superb company. It will be marvellous this evening – I can't wait. But then you face a long haul to February 9th. And I wanted to talk about that.

Remember that you're changing lives. At every performance.

You may find that you're performing this fairy tale while this country goes to war. Real bombs, real deaths. Does that make our work irrelevant or petty? Not at all. While the politicians send people out to kill or be killed and bomb the hell out of Iraq – you will be asserting the values of kindness and courage and creation. You are creating beauty for children – the most important audience of all.

These days I mostly write plays for children. I haven't totally given up on adults. But children come to the theatre with open minds, open imaginations and open hearts. They come to the theatre as an adventure.

Many are coming to the theatre for the first time. If they are delighted, they will always have a hunger for good theatre. If they are bored or disappointed – they won't want to come back. But they can't be bored or disappointed while you're working well. The story is beautiful, the music is beautiful, the sets are beautiful. At every performance – you will change lives.

I don't mean the children will all want to work in the theatre. But your performances will open doors – so that one child may decide to be a doctor, another to be an explorer, another to be a writer, another to marry the White Witch.

At every performance you will be faced by these people with open hearts. I wish you could see them come out of the theatre – they dance their way out.

Yesterday I met a family who had been delighted by your acting. They were from Colorado and the youngest was a little blonde girl called Georgia, about five or six years old. When I asked her which person in the play she liked best, she thought a bit, then said: the Unicorn. Yes, you Sasha. As the Unicorn you will act your part seriously and beautifully at every performance – for Georgia. And the rest of you will do the same. If you're ever tempted to fool around, sometime between now and February 9th – remember Georgia. Remember the Unicorn.

16. ON A GOOD DAY YOU CAN SEE GOD

Longing to see the sex life of JC. I intend writing a stage show called *Jesus Christ's Day Off* in which all sorts of *Carte Blanche* tricks (miracles) are used by the lad for pure joy purposes. (The Miracle of the Million Mars Bars; The Screwing of the Seven Thousand). Well, the Christians had their whack at warping my sensuality and fears. I'd rather have William Blake, Bessie Smith, Mark Twain, Houdini, Marie Lloyd, Max Miller and Duke Ellington.

Calderón de la Barca
or How I Learned To Stop Worrying
and Love the Spanish Golden Age

This introduction is not for scholars. They know far more about Calderón than I do. It is for those people who find themselves intimidated by the strangeness of Spain, even contemporary Spain, let alone the seventeenth-century Spain.

I felt that same nervousness only a few years ago. I'd stayed away from Spain all my life because of bloody Franco. When I first read about the plays of the Spanish Golden Age – from around 1500 to 1681, the period in which Calderón, Lope de Vega, Cervantes, Tirso de Molina and Rojas Zorrilla flourished – I was dumbfounded by the system of values, especially the 'Honour' system which seemed to dominate the drama. It was only when I began to read the plays thoroughly that I discovered that you have to know very little about such matters to understand many of the greatest plays. Honour is such a strange word in England these days. Good name and reputation are still far easier to handle.

But when you read or act or watch *The Mayor of Zalamea* you need to know about human beings, not about social codes. Of course, the more you know about the social background the more you'll understand and enjoy. But most of us live in a world which doesn't allow time for historical research in between work or looking for work and going to the theatre. *The Mayor of Zalamea* was the first Spanish play I attempted, using a literal translation by Gwenda Pandolfi, sticking very closely to the text, using a kind of syllabic verse. All the great Spanish plays are verse plays. That's what gives them their energy. A poetic play is like a river. A prose play is a road. Would you rather travel by riverboat or bus?

This was commissioned by the National Theatre. It was the first Spanish classic to be given a major stage production since World War Two. When I read the play for the second time I knew that given a half-decent staging, it must be popular. Michael Bogdanov's production was spare and strong and had at its centre a performance of pure gold by Michael Bryant. *The Mayor of Zalamea* proved that there is no difficulty for an English audience with at least one of the Golden Age plays. It started at the Cottesloe and transferred to the Olivier because more seats were needed.

After its success the National suggested another Calderón, *Life's a Dream*. But just as I was completing my version it was discovered that the Royal Shakespeare Company was about to stage a version of the same play by John Barton. I rang John, whom I didn't know at the time, to confirm that this was true, since the National had decided to scrap its plans. He is the most generous of bears and said something like: 'Come on over and I'll show you mine and you show me yours.' We both liked each other's versions. He'd solved problems I had been stumped by. I'd laid down some mean verse. John suggested mixing the versions together and that's what we did. He kept a kind of record of whose line was whose and it worked out about 46 per cent John, 46 per cent Adrian and eight lines which were a mixture of the two. His production was highly acclaimed both in Stratford and London and once again the availability of Spanish drama to an English audience was proved.

The Great Theatre of the World was commissioned by the Mediaeval Players. The metaphor of the play, in which God is a theatre director and the World is his put-upon stage manager, appealed to me strongly. So did the humour and the pathos and the poetic wonder of the play – it is a Christian play but a pretty undogmatic one, naturally, since Calderón could take it for granted that he had a Christian audience. Its morality tells us, among other things, to think deeply about how we live our lives. Its poetry shows us how to love each other and the planet. It shows how the world emerged out of chaos, how human beings arrived on the planet and how we should live our lives. It entertains us with personal comedies and tragedies, songs, jokes and, above all, poetry.

The theatre is a real world. This has advantages and disadvantages. One given factor for this production was that the Players have developed many circus skills like juggling and stilt-walking. We used this by giving the play an interlude halfway through in which, since the play is much possessed by death, skeletons danced and played, giant skeletons walked on bone-like stilts and juggler skeletons demonstrated their art with skulls and bones. Disadvantages – the Players' grant couldn't stretch to a complete cast. One character, I was told, had to be left out. I chose the one which I felt was least relevant to a modern audience, the character Discretion, who chooses a contemplative life. Don't blame me, blame Mrs Thatcher. I suppose I could have written back Discretion into the play for this published edition. I decided not to. This is a version for Philistine Britain where even a very funny and affecting play about eternal truths has to lose, if not a limb, then a few fingers in the cause of cost-effectiveness. Calderón lived from 1600 to

1681. To find out about his life and work, read his entry in *The Oxford Companion to Spanish Literature* and Gerald Brenan's wonderful *The Literature of the Spanish People.*

His work is sometimes characterised as formal, intellectual, spiritual, maybe somewhat cold. All these things are true, but there is far more to his plays. They're certainly not cold, they simply seem comparatively cool when you place them beside the red-hot passion of Lope de Vega. But there is a slow-burning passion in Calderón and also a lovely humour which is often forgotten. Lope de Vega (1562-1635) was surely a mixture of earth and fire. Calderón is air and water, a most beautiful fountain. And often, a fiery fountain.

Introduction to Adrian's Pedro Calderón de la Barca: Three Plays
published by Oberon Books in 1991

17. PULL THE PLUGS

There's one thing worse than your average rock musical and that's your average religious rock musical. Rock is good for bopping to and other practical purposes. Jazz goes further. Jazz surprises. If there's any amplified music in song theatre the volume must be turned way down otherwise the singers will have to use mikes. Why shouldn't they? Because the naked human voice is a creature of great beauty. I like to see it naked. Not passed through some buzzing sound system. Naked voice with endless varieties of unamplified instruments.

Worth trying, doll.

Theatre and Song

In the days when everyone lived in tribes, poetry was always something which was sung and danced, sometimes by one person, sometimes by the whole tribe. Songs always had a purpose – a courting song, a song to make the crops grow, a song to help or instruct the hunter of seals, a song to thank the sun. Later on, when poetry began to be printed, it took on airs. When the universities started studying verse instead of alchemy, poetry began to strut around like a duchess full of snuff. By the middle of the twentieth century very few British poets would dare to sing.

There's a natural hunger for songs. The enormous popularity of good musicals and some bad musicals underlines this. I'm not at all shocked when people point out that the most popular shows in London and New York are almost all musicals. I'm only shocked that 98 per cent of musicals are simply sugar-coated idiocy. There is no need for musicals to be stupid or shallow or sentimental.

People love to hear good songs. They love good plays. And a good play with good songs and good dancing seems too wonderful to be true. Plays and dances don't have to be stupid, although stupidity is easy to sell. The truth hurts. Since the Broadway musical is principally aimed at a wealthy audience, it is unlikely to offend that audience with anything more critical than a few jokes about rich people. The coach parties from New England will not flock down for stories which criticise the capitalist system itself.

There's often a difference between some poems and some lyrics. Lyrics tend to be less concentrated, partly because they have to work instantly and partly because they must allow room for the music to breathe, some work for the music to do.

I've been very lucky in my composers. My working method is usually this. To discuss with the composer what songs are needed. To write lyrics and read them aloud to the composer – just to indicate tone, possible rhythms and make the meaning of the lyric clear. I may rewrite at this point if the composer has good suggestions. Then I hand over the lyrics and go write some more. Often I've had to write to very tight deadlines. The only shortcut I've ever found in these circumstances, and I've used it very rarely, is to write lyrics to an existing tune and fail to inform the composer. I did this, for example, with Charlotte Corday's waltz in *Marat/Sade* which I wrote to the tune of 'The Blue Danube'.

I was born on October 24th 1932, so I was a kid during World War Two. I believe that World War Three began in 1945 when we dropped the atomic bomb on Hiroshima. That has been continuing ever since, in Malaysia, Aden, Vietnam, Zimbabwe, Czechoslovakia, Cyprus, Kenya, Suez, Hungary, Israel, Nicaragua and so on. The hope must be that it won't escalate. So all my songs have been written in wartime and they probably reflect it. And they are love songs because the main motive for writing them is love – the love of words, the love of listening to songs, the love of my family and friends for whom I write the songs and love for this poor planet and its living inhabitants, human and otherwise. But how the hell did I find myself writing plays with songs in a century like this? I've been bloody lucky, as you will see.

My mother loved the theatre and she took me to almost any play or show I wanted to see. Every season we would visit the Gilbert and Sullivan operas. I memorised most of W. S. Gilbert's lyrics, which I found endlessly funny and clever.

The big American musicals knocked me sideways. *Oklahoma!* came first. I still think 'The Surrey With The Fringe on Top' one of the sweetest love songs which never mentions love and 'I Cain't Say No' one of the funniest point numbers. *Annie Get Your Gun* I liked even better at the time, though it hasn't lasted so well. I was still in love with Broadway musicals when *Pal Joey* and *The Pajama Game* proved that they don't have to be sentimental. And then *Guys and Dolls* – one of the greatest theatre pieces of all time, ranked alongside *The Beggar's Opera* for its combination of daring plot, character, wit, sharp lyrics and perfect music. But mostly, despite *Sweeney Todd*, the Broadway product is mindless, toothless and self-regarding. The book, the story, is seen as a nuisance. The star descends a staircase to be greeted by a Hello Dollying chorus, an eternally recurring image…

As a teenager in the late Forties I was eccentric in my hobby – collecting records. Louis Armstrong, Danny Kaye, Dinah Shore, Duke Ellington, Fats Waller, Bing Crosby – whenever I could afford them, I bought them. At that time only about one in fifty teenagers shared this fascination. I even bought the *Melody Maker* along with the *New Statesman*, and from the *MM*, at the age of fourteen, learned for the first time about the extent of racism in the USA and the fact that it was growing in Britain.

And I listened to the words of the song. The standard hit song of the time was full of abstract words like devotion and emotion plus a few property moons and stars above – awful lyrics like tons of white mud. But the blues was full of concrete images – *Make me a pallet on your floor, If you see me comin', sash your window high* or *I went down to St James Infirmary, saw my baby there, laying on a long white table, so sweet, so cold, so bare*. It was true poetry and I knew it.

Some of the funny songs of the period like 'Tallahasse' or 'Accentuate the Positive' were good and witty. The old music hall songs often had flair and imagination. But at that time very few British poets were writing songs. Auden did some and MacNeice as well. But why weren't Dylan Thomas and George Barker writing lyrics for Duke Ellington to set?

Then came rock 'n' roll and the lyrics changed drastically as Tin Pan Alley was invaded by the forces of rhythm and blues. 'Blue Suede Shoes', 'Heartbreak Hotel', 'Great Balls of Fire', 'Blueberry Hill', 'Sweet Little Sixteen' – they were jumping with images of city life.

Chuck Berry's songs were heady with the fumes of fast cars and cheap perfume. They told rapid-fire stories – 'Come On, Maybelline' and, most amazing of all, 'The Promised Land' in which the singer tells of an extraordinary cross-country journey from Virginia to Los Angeles with accidents thrown in.

But my favourite song-writing combination of that era was the team of Jerry Leiber (lyrics), Mike Stoller (music) and The Coasters. The best Coasters records – 'Riots In Cell Block Number Nine', 'Searchin'', 'Yakety Yak', 'The Shadow Knows', 'What About Us?', 'Little Egypt', 'Shopping For Clothes' and 'D. W. Washburn' all seem to be sung by real people with real characters. Many of them, like 'What Is The Secret Of Your Success?' are three-minute dramas with more than one character. Why is there no boxed set of the complete Coasters?

Leiber/Stoller went on to write many fine songs, especially for Peggy Lee – you may know 'Is That All There Is?' but you should hear her extraordinary dark Leiber/Stoller LP called *Mirrors* which includes the wild version of 'Professor Hauptmann's Performing Dogs'.

Along came the Beatles and suddenly British singers were writing their own lyrics. As their confidence grew, they pushed back the frontiers of lyric writing to achieve wonders like 'Penny Lane', 'Come Together' and 'A Day In The Life'. If you asked me, I could write a book. But onward. After the break-up, John Lennon stripped down his style to write some of the greatest lyrics ever in songs like 'Mother'. This was naked poetry, frightening and true.

Since then many fine lyric writers have come and gone. The ones I have followed most avidly have been Paul Simon, Randy Newman and Bob Dylan. Lately I've been impressed with a lot of Elvis Costello, Sting and Peter Gabriel.

I'd love to write for singers like Joe Cocker or Madeline Bell, but somehow it never happened. Although I spent a couple of years writing about pop records, I concentrated on the lyrics and the beat and avoided as far as possible the sort of party contacts with the salesforce which you need to become a regular wordsmith.

In the past ten years I've been writing far fewer poems than I used to, mainly because most of my energy goes into my songs. Poetry is a bucket for carrying truth, and so are songs. I'm happy enough if I've got a bucket.

I'd started writing plays at the age of nine or ten. At my secondary school, Dauntsey's in Wiltshire, I met my greatest friend, Gordon Snell. The school ran an annual one-act play competition – you had to write your own – and the winning play won points for its House. Gordon and I collaborated on several of these plays. There was *A Friend Of Ours* in which a personified Death (in a wheelchair) invited a group of people to his country house. There was a blank verse melodrama in which I had to say: 'This bullet in my stomach is my life's result, The culmination of the sequence of my acts…' There was *The Third Ham* – a parody of *The Third Man* – which was banned by the school censors because of blasphemy and obscenity. Gordon and I took turns to direct and star in these dramas. One term he was playing Hamlet in the school play and I was Claudius, so we were barred from taking speaking parts in our last play. Thus we came to write *Cow Cow Bogey* – a Western epic entirely centred round a Charlestoning cow, played by Gordon and myself. But we didn't include songs in our plays. Song-writing started, for me, at Oxford, contributing parodies of pop songs to an anti-Royal, anti-establishment revue called *Bad Taste*.

I became a journalist – a reporter on the *Oxford Mail* and also its theatre reviewer. I began to learn about the use of songs in non-Broadway theatre. Joan Littlewood's Theatre Workshop was my delight. And I began to understand the song theatre of Brecht and, later, of John Arden.

I became committed to the idea of plays with songs, as opposed to musicals. I didn't want enormous budgets and compulsory, meaningless chorus lines. I didn't want songs designed for the hit parade rather than for dramatic effect, songs which had to be endlessly plugged in the show. What I wanted was *Oh! What A Lovely War*, Behan's *The Hostage*, Alan Plater's *Close the Coalhouse Door*, John McGrath's *The Fish In The Sea* and Brecht's *The Caucasian Chalk Circle*. What I wanted was the kind of music theatre which Alan Dossor created at the Liverpool Everyman and Richard Eyre at the Nottingham Playhouse, both directors in the Littlewood tradition. Eventually I worked with both of them. Alternative Music Theatre touches contemporary problems in the real world. It questions society and established values. It explores possibilities. It creates not only fun but disturbance.

The greatest problem in staging most of the shows that follow has been that British theatres aren't geared to plays with songs. Musicians have to be specially hired, and, at nearly all rehearsals, you only have the pianist. Sound systems are usually rusty and unreliable. Actors have to be auditioned endlessly and exhaustively. I've learned never to believe actors who say they can sing (or actors who say they can't).

What we need is a National Song Theatre. It will have a regular company of versatile musicians and actors who can all sing and dance. It will have several auditoriums with sound systems to equal those of rock groups. It will revive the best of music theatre from the past. It will create new plays with songs, both big and small. It will import music theatre from other countries, not just from the USA. It will constantly keep a touring company on the road. It will run its own theatre school. It will be built in Liverpool or Glasgow in the year 2024.

I once cornered Sir Roy Shaw, when he was head of the Arts Council, with this idea. He was enthralled and suggested I should come to the Arts Council headquarters and explain this to the people who specialised in such matters. I sent in a long memo and was invited in. There I met two men and a woman. The meeting lasted about an hour. One of the men arrived half an hour late. The other left for another meeting half an hour early. Neither of them gave any sign of having read my memo. I tried to explain but was constantly questioned by the woman, who had read the memo, not very thoroughly, and who told me she was going to act as a Devil's Advocate. That meant being as destructive as possible. Now the fact was I had come along with a serious enthusiasm knowing full well that I couldn't develop it by myself. I was looking for fellow enthusiasts to work out the possibilities of such a policy before searching for PROBLEMS. All the best people I've ever worked with, from Peter Brook to Sylvester McCoy, from Jonathan Pryce to John Fox, are not given to talking about PROBLEMS. They are interested in artistic vision and keen to share their visions and to help develop those of other people. The kind of theatre people who see problems everywhere are the soggy plodnik worrier place-men who wouldn't know a vision if it hit them on the head with an Ark of the Covenant.

Adapted introduction to Adrian's
Love Songs of World War Three, *published in 1988.*

18. BATHROOM THEATRE

I did a play today. With my wife. SHE: There's no lavatory paper. ME: Yes there is. In the bathroom. SHE: No there isn't. *(EXIT ME. ME finds six rolls hidden by chest of drawers in bathroom. ME takes two of them back to SHE.)* ME *(holding two rolls up like binoculars)*: I see no lavatory. SHE *(pleased)*: Where were they? *(ME sets up the ground-plan of the bathroom on the sitting-room floor, indicating the whereabouts of the chest of drawers and placing the two rolls in the correct position to play the part of the six rolls. ME acts out entering the bathroom worried. ME acts out delight at the discovery of the rolls.)* SHE: Why don't you go to the bathroom and rehearse the Finding of the Rolls in the Bathroom? *(Curtain.)* There's the Theatre of Everyday Life. 'I wouldn't pay good money to see that on a stage.' I'm not after your money, Greyface, however good it is. I do it for fun. Because I love her.

List of Plays

The Ledge libretto, music by Richard Rodney Bennett, Sadler's Wells Theatre, 1961.

The Persecution and Assassination of Jean-Paul Marat as Performed by the Inmates of Charenton Under the Direction of the Marquis de Sade translated and adapted from the play by Peter Weiss, music by Richard Peaslee, Royal Shakespeare Company at Aldwych Theatre, 1964.

The Magic Flute adapted from the libretto by Schikaneder and Giesecke, music by Mozart, Royal Opera House, 1966.

US music by Richard Peaslee, RSC at Aldwych Theatre, 1966.

The Criminals adapted from the play by José Triana, RSC at Aldwych Theatre, 1967.

Hotspot Saga music by Greg Stephens and Boris Howarth, Morecambe, 1968.

Move over, Jehovah or *The Man Who Shot Emily Bronte* music by Boris Howarth, National Association for Mental Health, Holland Park Comprehensive School, 1968.

Lash Me to the Mast! music by Boris Howarth and Greg Stephens, Grand Theatre, Lancaster, 1969.

Tamburlane the Mad Hen music by Tony Attwood, tour of primary schools, 1970.

Tyger: A Celebration of the Life and Work of William Blake music by Mike Westbrook, National Theatre at the New Theatre, 1971.

Man Friday music by Mike Westbrook, BBC TV 1972, 7:84 stage tour 1973, film 1975.

Mind Your Head music by Tony Haynes, Everyman Theatre, Liverpool, 1973. Music by Andy Roberts, Shaw Theatre, 1974.

The Government Inspector adapted from the play by Gogol, Nottingham Playhouse, 1974. National Theatre, 1985.

Mass Media Mash Dartington College of Arts, 1974.

Kardiff Rules Ok music by Geoff Pearson, Sherman Theatre, Cardiff, 1975.

The Free Mud Fair music by William York, The Island of Angels, Totnes, 1976.

The Fine Art of Bubble-Blowing music by Stanley Myers, BBC TV, 1975.

Total Disaster music by Andy Roberts, BBC TV, 1975.

A Seventh Man music by Dave Brown, Foco Novo tour and Hampstead Theatre, 1976.

Round the World in Eighty Days adapted from the novel by Jules Verne, music by Bill Scott, Nottingham Playhouse, 1977.

White Suit Blues adapted from works by Mark Twain, music by Mike Westbrook. Nottingham Playhouse Company in Nottingham, London and Edinburgh, 1977.

Houdini: A Circus-Opera libretto, music by Peter Schat, Royal Dutch Opera, Carre Theatre, Amsterdam, 1977.

Uppendown Mooney or *The Exploding Bear and the Blue River* music by Boris Howarth and Greg Stephens. Welfare State International at Hilltop, Wennington and on tour, 1978.

The White Deer adapted from the story by James Thurber, music by Ilona Sekacz, Unicorn Theatre, 1978.

In the Unlikely Event of an Emergency music by Stephen McNeff, South-West Music Theatre, 1979.

Hoagy, Bix and Wolfgang Beethoven Bunkhaus King's Head Theatre, London 1979.

Peer Gynt adapted from the play by Ibsen, music by Nick Bicat,
Oxford Playhouse, 1980.

Mowgli's Jungle music by Mike Westbrook, Contact Theatre,
Manchester, 1981.

The Mayor of Zalemea or *The Best Garotting Ever Done*, adapted from
the play by Calderón, National Theatre, London 1981.

Something Down There Is Crying, music by Andy Roberts, BBC TV,
1981.

You Must Believe All This music by Nick Bicat and Andrew Dickson,
Thames Television, 1981.

The Wild Animal Song Contest music by Andrew Dickson, Unicorn
Theatre, 1982.

Life's a Dream adapted from the play by Calderón, music by Guy
Woolfenden, RSC at The Other Place, 1983.

A Child's Christmas in Wales with Jeremy Brooks, adapted from a story
by Dylan Thomas. Great Lakes Theater Festival, Cleveland, 1982.

Raising the Titanic music by Luk Mishalle, Welfare State International,
London Docks, 1984.

The Tragedy of King Real music by Pete Moser, Welfare State
International film, 1984.

Cmon Everybody music by Pete Moser, tour and Tricycle Theatre,
1984.

The Great Theatre of the World adapted from the play by Calderón,
music from traditional ballads. Mediaeval Players, 1984.

Music by Andrew Dickson, Arcola Theatre, London 2007.

Animal Farm lyrics only, music by Richard Peaslee, National Theatre,
1984.

Asterix and the Great Divide lyrics only, music by Ilona Sekacz,
Unicorn Theatre, 1984.

Satie Day/Night music by Erik Satie, Lyric Hammersmith, 1986.

On the Loose music by Pete Moser and Boris Howarth, Welfare State International tour, 1986-7.

The Pied Piper music by Dominic Muldowney, National Theatre 1986-7 and 1987-8.

Love Songs of World War Three music by various composers, National Theatre, 1987.

The Last Wild Wood in Sector 88 music by Guy Woolfenden, Rugby Music Centre, 1987.

Mirandolina adapted from a play by Goldoni, Bristol Old Vic, 1987.

Woman Overboard music by Monty Norman, Palace Theatre, Watford 1988.

The Patchwork Girl of Oz music by Andy Roberts. Palace, Watford 1988.

Anna on Anna Theatre Workshop, Edinburgh 1988.

Fuente Ovejuna adapted from the play by Lope de Vega, music by Paddy Cunneen, National Theatre, 1989.

Triple Threat music by various composers, National Theatre , 1989.

The Snow Queen adapted from the story by Hans Christian Andersen, music by Richard Peaslee, New York State Theatre Institute, 1990.

Naming the Animals music by Phil Minton and Veryan Weston, Lancaster Literature Festival, 1991.

Vasilisa the Fair adapted from Russian folk tales, New York State Theatre Institue, 1991.

Unicorn Island music by Andrew Dickson, Dartington College of Arts, 1992.

The Blue music by Pete Moser, Fitzcarraldo Theatre Ship, Glasson Dock, Lancashire, 1992.

A New World and the Tears of the Indians music by Pete Moser, Nuffield Theatre, Southampton, 1992.

Meet the Baron Dartington College of Arts, 1993.

Sir Fool's Quest music by Andrew Dickson, PuppetCraft tour, 1994.

Tyger Two music by Mike Westbrook, Emerson College, Boston, 1995.

Tom Kitten and his Friends adapted from stories by Beatrix Potter, music by Steve McNeff, Unicorn Theatre, 1995.

Lost in a Mirror adapted from the play by Lope de Vega, Southwark Playhouse, 1995.

The Siege music by Andrew Dickson, various comprehensive schools, 1996-7.

The Little Violin music by Pete Moser, Tricycle Theatre, 1998.

The Lion, the Witch and the Wardrobe adapted from the novels by C.S. Lewis, music by Shaun Davey, Royal Shakespeare Theatre, Stratford-upon-Avon, 1998.

Start Again music by Pete Moser, Morecambe, 1998.

Jemima Puddleduck and her Friends adapted from stories by Beatrix Potter, music by Stephen McNeff, Unicorn Theatre, 1998.

The Heroes (trilogy) music by Andrew Dickson, Kageboushi Theatre Company, 1999.

The Mammoth Sails Tonight music by Pete Moser, Dream Factory, Warwick, 1999.

Alice in Wonderland and *Through the Looking Glass* adapted from the novels by Lewis Carroll, music by Terry Davies and Stephen Warbeck, Royal Shakespeare Theatre, Stratford-upon-Avon, 2001.

Peter Rabbit and His Friends adapted from stories by Beatrix Potter, music by Stephen McNeff, Unicorn Theatre, 2002.

Aladdin music by Andrew Dickson, Theatre on the Rock, Belfast, 2004.

King of Shadows adapted from the novel by Susan Cooper, New York State Theatre Institue, 2005.

Nobody Rides the Unicorn adapted from his own story with Sasha

Mitchell, music by Andrew Dickson, PuppetCraft tour, 2005.

Perseus and the Gorgon's Head music by Andrew Dickson. Puppetcraft tour, 2006.

The Fear Brigade music by Andrew Dickson, Global Village, 2006.

To the River music by Andy Roberts, BBC Radio 4, 2007.

Maudie and the Green Children music by Andy Roberts, Dundee Repertory Theatre, 2008.

The Jubilee Singers BBC Radio 4, 2010.

Plays as yet unperformed

Ahab based on *Moby Dick* by Herman Melville, music by Richard Peaslee.

Boris Godunov adapted from the play by Alexander Pushkin.

Everybody's Joey based on the life of Joseph Grimaldi

The Jubilee Singers stage version.

Just William or *England in Trouble* based on the novels by Richmal Crompton.

The Magic Faraway Tree based on the novel by Enid Blyton.

We music by Richard Peaslee.

Wings and the Child based on the life and work of E. Nesbit.

www.ingramcontent.com/pod-product-compliance
Ingram Content Group UK Ltd.
Pitfield, Milton Keynes, MK11 3LW, UK
UKHW031106020325
455687UK00007B/69